# SAFE AND DRUG FREE SCHOOLS

# SAFE AND DRUG FREE SCHOOLS

PATRICIA V. NOBLE (EDITOR)

Novinka Books
*New York*

**Senior Editors:** Susan Boriotti and Donna Dennis
**Coordinating Editor:** Tatiana Shohov
**Office Manager:** Annette Hellinger
**Graphics:** Wanda Serrano
**Editorial Production:** Vladimir Klestov, Matthew Kozlowski and Maya Columbus
**Circulation:** Ave Maria Gonzalez, Vera Popovic, Luis Aviles, Raymond Davis, Melissa Diaz and Jeannie Pappas
**Communications and Acquisitions:** Serge P. Shohov
**Marketing:** Cathy DeGregory

*Library of Congress Cataloging-in-Publication Data*

Safe and drug free schools / Patricia V. Noble (editor).
    p. cm.
   Includes index.
   ISBN: 1-59033-494-9.
   1. Students—Drug use—United States—Prevention. 2. Youth—Drug Use—United States—Prevention. 3. School violence—United States—Prevention. 4. Drug abuse—Study and teaching—Law and legislation—United States. 5. Drug abuse—United States—Prevention—Finance. 6. United States. Safe and Drug-Free Schools and Communities Act. I. Noble, Patricia V.

HV5824.Y68 S237 2002
371.7'84'0973—dc21

                                                                               2002035807

Copyright © 2002 by Novinka Books, An Imprint of
        Nova Science Publishers, Inc.
        400 Oser Ave, Suite 1600
        Hauppauge, New York 11788-3619
        Tele. 631-231-7269             Fax 631-231-8175
        e-mail: Novascience@earthlink.net
        Web Site: http://www.novapublishers.com

All rights reserved. No part of this book may be reproduced, stored in a retrieval system or transmitted in any form or by any means: electronic, electrostatic, magnetic, tape, mechanical photocopying, recording or otherwise without permission from the publishers.

The authors and publisher have taken care in preparation of this book, but make no expressed or implied warranty of any kind and assume no responsibility for any errors or omissions. No liability is assumed for incidental or consequential damages in connection with or arising out of information contained in this book.

This publication is designed to provide accurate and authoritative information with regard to the subject matter covered herein. It is sold with the clear understanding that the publisher is not engaged in rendering legal or any other professional services. If legal or any other expert assistance is required, the services of a competent person should be sought. FROM A DECLARATION OF PARTICIPANTS JOINTLY ADOPTED BY A COMMITTEE OF THE AMERICAN BAR ASSOCIATION AND A COMMITTEE OF PUBLISHERS.

*Printed in the United States of America*

# CONTENTS

**Preface** vii

**Chapter 1** The Safe and Drug-Free Schools and Communities
Act: Reauthorization and Appropriations 1
*Edith Fairman Cooper*

**Chapter 2** The Safe and Drug-Free
Schools and Communities Act 9
*Jennifer A. Neisner*

**Chapter 3** The Safe and Drug-Free Schools
and Communities Program 19
*Cecilia Oregón Echeverria*

**Chapter 4** The Safe and Drug-Free Schools and
Communities Program: Background and Context 41
*Edith Fairman Cooper*

**Index** 75

# PREFACE

Illegal drug use is a recurrent problem across the nation, but at particular risk are the nation's youth. Studies have shown that among children, drug use begins with the abuse of legal substances (i.e. tobacco and alcohol) before graduating to illegal drugs, with marijuana generally the first. Along with drug abuse, violence is another danger the nation's young people must face, be it drug motivated or the result of other behavioral problems. Schools are considered prime places to head off these two threats through education about abstaining from drugs and controlling violent tendencies. In 1996, the Department of Education began overseeing the Safe and Drug-Free Schools and Communities Act, which funds both state and national drug and violence prevention programs. Unfortunately, follow-up studies have revealed mixed results to the national program. The Education Department, though, is considering steps to strengthen and improve this critical program.

This book examines and evaluates the Safe and Drug-Free Schools and Communities Act and its programs, placing the measure in a background context and looking at its financial and administrative structures. Given the major problems of drug abuse and violence threatening to overwhelm children, these studies make for a timely analysis of an important issue.

*Chapter 1*

# THE SAFE AND DRUG-FREE SCHOOLS AND COMMUNITIES ACT: REAUTHORIZATION AND APPROPRIATIONS

*Edith Fairman Cooper*

## ABSTRACT

The 107th Congress considered and approved reauthorization legislation to extend and amend the Elementary and Secondary Education Act (ESEA) and the Safe and Drug-Free Schools and Communities Act (SDFSCA). Also, legislation to make FY2002 appropriations to continue funding for the program was approved. The President signed both measures into law. The President has released his FY2003 budget request for the SDFSC and other federal programs. He has proposed $644,250,000 for the SDFSC program, which is a $102,500,000 decrease of the FY2002 appropriation. It would eliminate three activities under national programs - mentoring, community services for expelled or suspended students, and alcohol abuse reduction.

## MOST RECENT DEVELOPMENTS

For FY2003, the President has requested $644,250,000 for the SDFSC program. On January 8, 2002, the President signed H.R. 1, the No Child Left Behind Act, into law (P.L.107-110). It amends SDFSCA as Part A of Title

IV - 21th Century Schools, FY2002 appropriations, signed into law (P.L. 107-116) on January 10, 2002, provided a total of $746,750,000 for the SDFSC program. Of this sum, $472,017,000 are for state grants, $34,733,000 for national programs, $10,000,000 for Project SERV (School Emergency Response to Violence), $37,500,000 for the National Coordinator Initiative, $100,000,000 for the Safe Schools/Healthy Students initiative, $17,500,000 for mentoring programs, $50,000,000 for community service for expelled or suspended students, and $25,000,000 for alcohol abuse reduction.

## INTRODUCTION

The authorization for the Safe and Drug-Free Schools and Communities Act expired on September 30, 2000. In the 107th Congress, legislation was considered and approved for reauthorization of the Act. This report discusses the SDFSCA reauthorization and appropriations to fund the SDFSCA program.

## THE SAFE AND DRUG-FREE SCHOOLS & COMMUNITIES PROGRAM: AUTHORIZATIONS

The No Child Left Behind Act (P.L. 107-110), amends and reauthorizes SDFSCA as Part A of Title IV – 21st Century Schools. It authorizes funds for the SDFSCA program, which is the federal government's major initiative to prevent drug abuse violence in and around schools. It awards state grants by formula to outlying areas, state educational agencies (SEAs), and local educational agencies (LEAs) in all 50 states, the District of Columbia (DC) and the Commonwealth of Puerto Rico. Also, funds go to a state's Chief Executive Officer (Governor) for creating programs to deter youth from using drugs and committing violent acts in schools. National programs are supported through discretionary funds for a variety of national leadership projects designed to prevent drug abuse and violence among all educational levels, from preschool through the postsecondary level.

## State Grants

For FY2002, $650 million was authorized for state grants and such sums as necessary for each succeeding fiscal year through FY2007. Of the funds authorized, 1% or $4,750,000 (whichever is greater) is reserved for Guam, American Samoa, the Virgin Islands, and the Commonwealth of the Northern Mariana Islands; 1% or $4,750,000 (whichever is greater) is reserved for the Secretary of the Interior to administer programs for Indian youth; and 0,2% is reserved to provide programs for native Hawaiians. The remaining funds are distributed to the states, DC, and Puerto Rico, by a formula of 50% based on school-aged population and 50% based on ESEA Title I, Part A concentration grants for the preceding fiscal year. No state receives less than the greater of one-half of 1% (0,5%) of the total allotted to all of the states or the amount for FY2001, under prior law. State grant funds in any amount may be redistributed to other states if the Secretary determines that a state will not be able to use the funds within 2 years of the initial award. Also, a limitation is included stipulating that funds appropriated for national programs may not be increased unless state grant funding is at least 10% more than the previous fiscal year's appropriation.

Of the total state allotment, 20% goes to the Governor to award competitive grants and contracts to LEAs, community-based groups, other public entities, private groups and associations. The Governor may not use more than 3% of the funds for administrative costs.

An SEA must distribute at least 93% of its allotment to LEAs for drug and violence prevention and education programs and activities. Of those funds, 60% are based on the relative amount LEAs received under ESEA Title I, Part A for the previous fiscal year, and 40% are based on public and private school enrollments. Also, of the amount received from the state, LEAs may use not more than 2% for administrative costs.

SEAs may use up to 3% of its allotment for administering the program. In FY2002, they may use in addition to the 3% administrative costs, 1% of the state's allotment (minus funds reserved for the Governor) to implement a uniform management information and reporting system (UMIRS). Funds may be used directly or through grants and contracts to create the UMIRS, which is designed to collect information on truancy rates; the incidence, seriousness, and frequency of violence and drug-related crimes that result in suspending and expelling students in elementary and secondary schools in a state; the kinds of curricula, programs, and services provided by the Governor, SEAs, LEAs, and other fund recipients; and the incidence and prevalence of drug use and violence among minors, age of onset of such behavior, and the perception of health risk and social disapproval for such behavior. SEAs may use not more than 5% of allotted funds for state activities for planning, developing, and implementing capacity building; providing technical assistance and training, evaluation, and program improvement services; and for coordinating activities for LEAs, community-based groups, and other public and private entities.

## National Programs

The authorization for national program was such sums as necessary for FY2002 through FY2007. Funds available under national programs allow the ED Secretary to consult with the HHS Secretary, the Director of the Office of National Drug Control Policy (ONDCP), and the Attorney General to administer programs aimed at preventing violence and illegal drug use among students and promoting their safety and discipline. Also, from national program funds, up to $2 million may be reserved for evaluating the national impact of the SDFSC program, and an amount necessary is reserved to continue the Safe Schools/Healthy Students initiative.[1] In FY 1999, the National Coordinator Initiative was created under national programs allowing LEAs to recruit, hire, and train persons to serve as SDFSC program coordinators in middle schools. ED officials believed that middle school students were at the age where they were most likely to begin experimenting with drugs and becoming more involved in violence and crime. H.R. 1 continues this permissive activity by expanding coverage for national coordinators to serve as drug prevention and school safety program coordinators in all schools with drug and safety problems.

National program funds may be made available as formula grants to states for administering programs that require students expelled or suspended from school to perform community service (see below for FY2002 appropriations provided for this activity). Grants would be made to states with 50% of allotted funds based on school-aged population and 50% based on ESEA Title I, Part A concentration grants for the preceding fiscal year. No state would receive less than one-half of 1% (0,5%) of the total allotted to all of the states. Competitive grants may be awarded, in consultation with the Administrator of the Substance Abuse and Mental Health Services Administration (SAMHSA, within HHS), to LEAs allowing school districts

---

[1] This initiative is funded jointly with HHS and the Department of Justice to assist school districts and communities in developing and implementing community-wide projects in order to create safe and drug-free schools and encourage healthy childhood development.

to develop and implement programs to reduce alcohol abuse in secondary schools (see below for FY2002 appropriations provided for this activity). In addition, grants may be awarded to LEAs, non-profit community-based groups, or to a partnership between an LEA and such an organization for assistance in creating and supporting mentoring programs and activities for children with greatest need (see below for FY2002 appropriations provided for this activity).

Other permissive initiatives authorized under national programs include allowing the ED Secretary to make grants to LEAs and community-based groups to assist localities most directly affected by hate crimes; creating a School Security Technology and Resource Center at the Sandia National Laboratories in partnership with the National Law Enforcement and Corrections Technology Center-Southeast and the National Center for Rural Law Enforcement in Little Rock, Arkansas, to be administered by the Attorney General as a resource for LEAs to assess school security, develop security technology, evaluate and implement such security, and to provide technical assistance for improving school security, and establishing a National Center for School and Youth Safety to be jointly created by the ED Secretary and the Attorney General to provide emergency assistance to local communities in response to school safety crises, to establish an anonymous student hotline so students can report possible violent behavior, to provide consultation to the public regarding school safety, to compile information about best practices related to school violence prevention, and to provide outreach to rural and impoverished communities.

## APPROPRIATIONS AND A FUNDING HISTORY

The conference agreement on the FY2002 appropriations for the Departments of Labor, Health and Human Services, and Education, provides funding to continue provisions of the SDFSC program. A total of $746,750,000 was appropriated for various authorities under the program. Of this sum, $472,017,000 are for state grants, $34,733,000 for national programs, $10,000,000 for Project SERV (School Emergency Response to Violence),[2] $37,500,000 for the National Coordinator Initiative, $100,000,000 for the Safe Schools/Healthy Students (SS/HS) initiative, $17,500,000 for mentoring programs, $50,000,000 for community service

---

[2] Conferees on the legislation stipulated that the availability of funds for the two emergency activities be extended through September 30, 2003.

for expelled or suspended students, and $25,000,000 for alcohol abuse reduction.

For FY2003, the President has requested $644,250,000 for the SDFSC program. Of this sum, $472,017,000 are requested for state grants and $172,233,000 for national program activities. This request is a $102,500,000 decrease of the FY2002 appropriation. It eliminates three activities under national programs - mentoring, community services for expelled or suspended students, and alcohol abuse reduction.

Table 1 presents a 7-year appropriation funding history for the program.

## THE GUN-FREE SCHOOLS ACT

The Gun-Free Schools Act, which was Title XIV, Part F of the ESEA, was incorporated as part of SDFSC because of its close relationship with the SDFSC program. This provision calls for each state receiving funds under the No Child Left Behind Act to have a law that requires LEAs to expel for 1 year any student bringing a weapon to school. The chief administering officer of an LEA, however, can modify the expulsion requirement on a case-by-case basis.

## Table 1. SDFSC Appropriations Funds, FY1997-FY2003, by Grant Program (in thousands)

| Program | FY1997 | FY1998 | FY1999 | FY2000[a] | FY2001 | FY2002 | FY2003 Pres. Budget Request |
|---|---|---|---|---|---|---|---|
| State Grants | $555,978 | $531,000 | $441,000 | $439,250 | $439,250 | $472,017[b] | $472,017 |
| National Programs | 0 | $25,000 | $27,003 | $29,023 | $28,000 | $34,733 | $45,000 |
| Project SERV | - | - | - | 0 | $10,000 | $10,000 | $10,000 |
| Coordinator Initiative | - | - | $35,000 | $50,000 | $50,000 | $37,500 | $17,233 |
| SS/HS | - | - | $62,997 | $81,727 | $117,000 | $100,000 | $100,000 |
| Mentoring | - | - | - | - | - | $17,500 | 0 |
| Community Service… | - | - | - | - | - | $50,000 | 0 |
| Alcohol Abuse Reduction | - | - | - | - | - | $25,000 | 0 |
| Total Funding | $555,978 | $556,000 | $566,000 | $600,000 | $644,250 | $746,750 | $644,250 |

Source: U.S. Department of Education Budget Service and Conference Report 107-342, Making Appropriations for the Departments of L-HHS-ED and Related Agencies for the Fiscal Year Ending September 30, 2002, December 19, 2001, p.124.

[a] FY2002 funds reflect the requirement that agencies reduce their FY2000 appropriation by 0.38%. ED rescinded a portion of the state grant appropriation (from the initial appropriation of $445 million by $5.7 million).

[b] The SDFSC is a forward-funded program. Total funds usually are available from July 1 of the fiscal year appropriated through September 30 of the following fiscal year. For FY2002, as for FY2000 and FY2001, the state grant appropriation was split. Of the annual appropriation, $142,017,000 will become available on July 1, 2002, and remain available through September 30, 2003. The remaining allotment, $330,000,000 will become available October 1, 2002, and remain available through September 30, 2003.

*Chapter 2*

# THE SAFE AND DRUG-FREE SCHOOLS AND COMMUNITIES ACT

*Jennifer A. Neisner*

## SUMMARY

The Safe and Drug-Free Schools and Communities Act (SDFSCA) funds both grants to the states and national programs to support substance abuse education and violence prevention activities. The Omnibus Consolidated Appropriations Act, 1997 (P.L. 104-208, H.R. 3610), signed into law September 30, 1996, provides the SDFSCA with $555.9 million for FY1997, $90 million more than the program received in FY1996, and $15.9 million for grants to states and provides no funds for SDFSC national programs.

The Drug-Free Schools and Communities Act was established by the 1986 Anti-Drug Abuse Act (P.L. 99-570). It has been amended several times: by the Hawkins/Stafford Elementary and Secondary School Improvement Amendments of 1988 (P.L. 100-297), the 1988 Anti-Drug Abuse Act (P.L. 100-690), the Drug-Free Schools and Communities Act Amendments of 1989 (P.L 101-226), and the Crime vvvv (P.L. 101-647). The Improving America's Schools Act of 1994 (P.L 103-382), among other things, added violence prevention to the program's original emphasis on substance abuse education.

## GRANTS TO STATES

Table 1 shows how program funds were distributed in FY1996. Funds for the Act are appropriated separately for the state grants and national programs. Funds appropriated for the state grants are distributed as follows: 1% to the Territories (Guam, American Samoa, the Virgin Islands, and the Commonwealth of the Northern Mariana Islands); 1% to the Secretary of the Interior to carry out programs for Indian youth; $1,000,000 for a national impact evaluation; and 0.2% for programs for native Hawaiians. The remainder is distributed to the states, the District of Columbia, and the Commonwealth of Puerto Rico, half on the basis of school-aged population and half on the basis of grants under part A of Chapter I of Title I of the Elementary and Secondary Education Act (ESEA) as amended. No state receives less than 0.5% of the amount allotted to all the states. The state and local educational agencies (LEAs) of each state receive 80% of the state's grant under the program for drug and violence prevention activities; the Office of the Governor receives 20%.

## ALLOCATIONS TO STATE EDUCATION AGENCIES

The state grants program is forward-funded, meaning that grants used to fund programs during the 1996-1997 school year were distributed to the states during the summer of 1996. Of the funds allocated to each SEA, 5% may be used by the agency for training and technical assistance in drug and violence prevention and to address violence associated with prejudice and intolerance; curricular materials; programs for Local Education Agencies (LEAs) and demonstration projects in drug and violence prevention; assistance to economically disadvantaged or sparsely populated areas; and evaluation activities. A state may use not more than 4% of the SEA grant for administration. Of the remaining funds allocated to the SEA, at least 91% is distributed to LEAs, as follows: 70% to LEAs based on the relative enrollments in public and private nonprofit elementary and secondary schools within the boundaries of such agencies; and 30% to LEAs that the SEA determines have the greatest need for additional funds to carry out drug and violence prevention programs. Where appropriate and consistent with a state's need assessment, not less than 25% of this amount is distributed to LEAs located in rural and urban areas; such sums may be distributed to up to 10% of the LEAs in the state, or five such agencies, whichever is greater.

Table 1. Allocation of funds, FY1996

| Expenditure Category | Amount (FY1996 appropriation in thousands) | Percentage share of total |
|---|---|---|
| *Total* | $465,971 | 100.0% |
| National programs | 24,993 | 5.4 |
| State grants program | 440,978 | 94.6 |
| Set-aside for territories (1% of state grants) | 4,409 | 0.9 |
| Set-aside for programs for Indian youth (1% of state grants) | 4,409 | 0.9 |
| Set-aside for programs for Native Hawaiians (0.2% of state grants) | 882 | 0.2 |
| Set-aside for evaluations | 1,000 | 0.2 |
| *State grants to governors and State Educational Agencies (SEAs)* | 430,278 | 92.3 |
| Amounts to Governors (20% of grants to Governors and SEAs) | 86,056 | 18.4 |
| (Minimum share to law enforcement education partnerships (10% of Governor's share)) | (8,605) | (1.8) |
| (Maximum share for administration (5% of Governor's share) | (4,303) | (0.9) |
| Amount to SEAs (80% of grants to Governors and SEAs) | 344,224 | 73.7 |
| (Maximum share to be used by SEAs (9% of SEA share)) | (30,980) | (6.6) |
| (Maximum share for SEA administration (4% of the funds reserved for SEAs)) | (1,239) | (0.3) |
| (Minimum share to be allocated to Local Education Agencies (LEAs) (91% of the SEA share)) | (313,245) | (67.0) |
| (Portion allocated to high-need areas (30% of LEA share)) | (93,974) | (20.1) |
| (Portion allocated on enrollments (70% of LEA share)) | (219,272) | (46.9) |

**Source:** The Department of Education, Budget Justifications.

In determining which LEAs have the greatest need for additional funds, the SEA considers data for LEAs in such areas as rates of youth alcohol or drug use; victimization of youth by violence and crime; arrests and convictions of youth for violent or substance abuse-related crime; extent of illegal gang activity; violence associated with prejudice and intolerance; referrals of youth to substance abuse treatment and rehabilitation programs, or to juvenile court; and reported cases of child abuse and domestic violence.

A LEA uses SDFSCA funds to adopt and carry out a comprehensive drug and violence prevention program designed to prevent the use, possession, and distribution of tobacco, alcohol, and illegal drugs by students, and the illegal use, possession, and distribution of such substances by employees. Such a program would also prevent violence, promote school safety, and create a disciplined environment conducive to learning. The program would promote the involvement of parents and coordination with community groups and agencies. A comprehensive drug and violence prevention program may include: (1) drug prevention and education programs that address the consequences of the use of illegal drugs, promote a sense of individual responsibility, and provide information about effective techniques for resisting peer pressure to use illegal drugs; (2) drug prevention programs which emphasize students' sense of individual responsibility; (3) drug prevention and education programs that address the consequences of violent and disruptive behavior, sexual harassment and abuse, and victimization associated with prejudice and intolerance; (4) violence prevention programs for school-aged youth which emphasize student's sense of individual responsibility; (5) professional development for teachers and other staff, (6) before- and after-school programs; (7) Drug Abuse Resistance Education (DARE) programs, including classroom instruction by uniformed law enforcement officers, and (8) evaluation of such activities.

An LEA may spend 20% of its SDFSCA funds for the support of "safe zones of passage" for students between home and school, and for the acquisition and installation of metal detectors and hiring of security personnel, but only if it has not received any other federal funding for such activities.

## ALLOCATIONS TO GOVERNORS

The funds allocated to the Office of the Governor are used for grants to or contracts with parent and community groups and organizations, and other public and private nonprofit entities for local drug and violence prevention activities. Priority is to be given to programs and activities that serve children and youth who are not normally served by state or LEAs; or populations that need special services or additional resources (such as preschoolers, youth in juvenile detention facilities, runaway or homeless children and youth, pregnant and parenting teenagers, and school dropouts).

In general, grants and contracts are used for such programs and activities as: (1) disseminating information about drug and violence prevention; (2) training parents, law enforcement and judicial officials, social and health service providers, and community leaders, (3) developing and implementing community-based programs that the link community resources with schools and integrated services; (4) planning and implementing activities that coordinate the efforts of state agencies with efforts of the SEA and its LEAs; (5) activities to protect students traveling to and from school; (6) before- and after-school programs that encourage drug- and violence-free lifestyles; (7) activities that promote the awareness of and sensitivity to alternatives to violence; (8) developing and implementing strategies to prevent and reduce violence associated with prejudice and intolerance; (9) developing and implementing strategies to prevent illegal gang activity; (10) coordinating and conducting community-wide violence and safety assessments and surveys; (11) service-learning projects that encourage drug- and violence-free lifestyles; and (12) evaluating such programs and activities.

At least 10% of the amount allocated to the Office of the Governor is to be used for grants to law enforcement agencies (including district attorneys) in consortium with LEAs or community-based agencies for law enforcement education partnerships. These partnerships carry out such drug abuse and violence prevention activities as: (1) Project DARE and other programs which provide classroom instruction by uniformed law enforcement officials; (2) Project Legal Lives and other programs in which district attorneys provide classroom instruction in the law and legal system which emphasizes interactive learning techniques, such as mock trial competitions; (3) partnerships between law enforcement and child guidance professionals; and (4) before- and after-school activities. Not more than 5% of the Governor's allocation may be used for administrative costs.

## NATIONAL PROGRAMS

National programs under the SDFSCA provide funds for a variety of programs designed to prevent the illegal use of drugs and violence among students at all educational levels. The national authority, as amended by P.L. 103-382, replaces previous authority for grants to institutions of higher education for model demonstrations and postsecondary prevention programs, programs for Indian youth and for Hawaiian natives, regional centers, school personnel training grants, emergency grants, and other discretionary federal activities. The Administration's FY 1997 budget request included $25 million for national programs. Based on the conferees' statement that the best use of federal substance abuse prevention funds is in the classroom, P.L. 104-208, the Omnibus Consolidated Appropriation for 1997, provides no funding for national programs. The conference report on P.L.104-208 (H.Rept. 104-863) does, however, state that Congress may consider reprogramming some of the state grant funds for national programs if the Secretary of Education feels such programs are sufficiently important.

National program funds have used for such activities as: (1) model programs for training of school personnel, parents, and members of the community; (2) demonstrations of innovative approaches to drug and violence prevention; (3) direct services to school systems with especially severe drug and violence programs; (4) financial and technical assistance to institutions of higher education for model drug prevention and campus safety programs; (5) grants to LEAs and community-based organizations to provide assistance to localities most directly affected by hate crimes; (6) drug and violence program evaluation; and (7) other federal initiatives that address unmet national needs relating to the purposes of law, including development and disseminating model curricula and other drug and violence prevention information and materials.

## PROGRAM FUNDING

Since 1987 the Safe and Drug-free Schools program has received over $5.1 billion. As table 2 indicates, appropriations for the program increased steadily during its early history before declining in the mid-1990's. Continued support for the program was uncertain for fiscal years 1995 and 1996. In early 1995, the program was threatened with a significant rescission in already appropriated FY1995 funds. In FY1996, Congress recommended providing less than the program had historically received. In both years, however, funding levels ultimately remained fairly constant as compared to FY 1994 funding.

**Table 2. Drug-Free Schools and Communities Act-Appropriations, FY 1987-1997 (dollars in thousands)**

| Fiscal year | Grants to states | Other [a] | Total |
|---|---|---|---|
| 1987 | $161,046 | $38,954 | $200,000 |
| 1988 | 191,480 | 38,296 | 229,776 |
| 1989 | 287,730 | 66,770 | 354,500 |
| 1990 | 437,881 | 101,319 | 539,200 |
| 1991 | 497,709 | 95,591 | 593,300 |
| 1992 | 507,663 | 116,300 | 623,963 |
| 1993 | 498,565 | 99,802 | 598,367 |
| 1994 | 369,500 | 117,662 | 487,162 |
| 1995 | 440,981 | 25,000 | 465,981 [b] |
| 1996 | 440,978 | 24,993 | 465,971 |
| 1997 | 555,978 | --- | 555,978 |

[a] until FY 1995 included personal training, national programs, and emergency grants, for FY1995, FY1996 and FY1997, includes national programs only.
[b] Amount reflects rescission of $15.981 million from the FY1995 appropriation.

The FY 1997 appropriation of $555.9 million is an increase of $90 million over the FY 1996 funding level and $15.9 million more that the President's FY 1997 request for the program. In its report on the FY 1997 Departments of Labor/HHS/Education appropriations bill (H.R.3577., H.Rept. 104-659), the House Committee on Appropriations provided funds for the state grants program but terminated funding for national programs, stating that it expected the Education Department to "employ its general authorities to fund the highest priority projects and activities" authorized under the national program. The Committee also expressed concern that despite program obligations of over $400 million per year since 1990, drug use by teens, which declined between 1985 and 1992, is again on the rise, and directs that state grant funds be used to "promote a 'no-use' message and support a 'no-use curricula.'"

# EVALUATING OF THE DRUG-FREE SCHOOLS PROGRAM

Federally supported surveys such as the National Household Survey on Drug Abuse (NHSDA) and the National High School Seniors Survey on Drug Abuse reported declines in illicit drug use between 1985 and 1992.

According to the NHSDA, the percentage of young people who had ever used an illicit drug dropped from 27.4% in 1985 to 15.1% in 1992. Similarly, the percent of current drug users (defined as having used an illicit drug within the past month) dropped from 13.2% in 1985 to 5.3% in 1992. However, it is difficult to know whether to attribute those changes to any particular program or to an overall national change in attitude toward drug use. Although the NHSDA notes that the rate of use has remained fairly steady in the overall population since 1992, the study shows rate of current use among youth age 12-17 has more than doubled (from 5.3% in 1992 to 10.9% in 1995), including large increases in the rate of current marijuana use (from 3.4% to 8.2%), and the cocaine use (0,3% to 0,8%). During this time there has also been an increase in the percent of young people having tired hallucinogens, inhalants, methamphetamine, or heroin. Additionally, these surveys show the percent of teens who disapprove of drug use or perceive it to be risky or harmful has declined significantly.

Research on the effectiveness of specific substance abuse prevention activities has been inconclusive. Some programs have demonstrated short-term success in improving students' awareness of the dangerous consequences of illicit drug use, but have had little apparent long-term impact on student behavior on drug use. The Office of Technology Assessment (OTA), in a 1991 report on adolescent health,[1] concluded from a review of efforts to prevent or delay the onset of adolescent illicit drug use that most prevention programs targeted at individuals "have yet failed to make a compelling case for their effectiveness." Some models, according to OTA, "show some positive effects in delaying increases in drug use, but the effects are generally small. Whether these models are of much practical significance in reducing drug use among adolescents in debatable." The OTA report, however, also concluded that some substance abuse prevention programs that produce little change in adolescents' use of alcohol and drugs, may be effective in other important respects, such as enhancing general life skills in such areas as social competence and decision making, and increasing knowledge about a range of psychoactive substances and possible psychological and developmental effects. The General Accounting Office (GAO) in a 1990 survey on school-based programs[2] concluded that, while evaluations of such programs generally have lacked needed scientific rigor

---

[1] U.S. Congress. Office of Technology Assessment. *Adolescent Health—Volume II: Background and the Effectiveness of Selected Prevention and Treatment Services.* OTA-H-466, November 1991. Washington, GPO, 1991. P. II-544.

[2] U.S. Congress. General Accounting Office. *Drug Education: School-Based Programs Seen as Useful but Impact Unknown.* GAO/HRD-91-27, November 1990. Washington, GPO, 1990.

and as a result offer little information on what works, "the message of drug and alcohol dangers is reaching the children." In the opinion of the both students and principals, according to GAO's discussions in 18 schools, drug and alcohol abuse among school-age children would be worse without the federally funded program.

The Department of Education does not yet have a formal evaluation of the impact of the Drug-Free Schools and Communities program. However, a recent report by the Department's Inspector General found that activities carried out under the Drug-Free School and Communities Act "clearly discouraged drug use." In 1990 the Department initiated an in-dept 5-year study of the effectiveness of school-based prevention programs, the results of which should be available in late 1996.

*Chapter 3*

# THE SAFE AND DRUG-FREE SCHOOLS AND COMMUNITIES PROGRAM

## *Cecilia Oregón Echeverria*

### ABSTRACT

Reducing youth drug use is one of the major goals of the 1998 National Drug Control Strategy. The Safe and Drug-Free Schools and Communities Act (SDFSCA), administered by the Department of Education (ED), funds both grants to the States and National Programs to support substance abuse education and violence prevention activities. The SDFSC program received $566 million for FY1999, with $441 million of that total used for state grants, $90 million for the National Programs and $35 million for the Coordinator Initiative.

### SUMMARY

Long-term studies of drug use suggest that children most often begin to use drugs at about age 12 or 13, moving from the illicit use of legal substances, such as tobacco, alcohol, and inhalants, to the use of illegal drugs. Marijuana is usually the first illicit drug used. The percent of adolescents using drugs more than doubled between 1992 and 1996. While the rate decreased slightly between 1996 and 1997, surveys show children are initiating drug use at earlier ages. In response, the Office of National

Drug Control Strategy (ONDCP) has made educating and enabling the nation's youth to reject illegal drugs, alcohol, and tobacco its first goal. Schools are though to be critical to motivation children to abstain from drug use: they offer the opportunity to reach all young people, and also serve as important settings for educating specific subpopulations at risk drug use, such as children with behavioral problems or learning disabilities, or those who are potential drop-outs.

The Safe and Drug-Free Schools and Communities Act (SDFSCA), administered by the Department of Education (ED), funds both grants to the states and national programs to support substance abuse education and violence prevention activities. Established by the 1986 Anti-Drug Abuse Act (P.L. 99-570), the Act has been amended several times, most recently by The Improving America's Schools Act of 1994 (P.L. 103-382) which, among other things, added violence prevention to the program's original emphasis on substance abuse education. The SDFSCA is authorized through FY 1999.

The SDFSCA encourages cooperation among schools, communities, parents, and governmental agencies to prevent substance use among children and adolescents. Grants are distributed to states based primarily on the number of school-age youth. State Education Agencies (SEAs) receive 80% of the total state allotment, while Governors' offices receive 20%. The majority of the state grant is passed on to Local Education Agencies (LEAs), with SEAs required to target 30% of their funds, to high-need districts.

The FY1999 appropriation for the SDFSC program is $566 million ($441 million for state grants, $90 million for national programs, and $35 million for a new Coordinator Initiative). Initiative funding will be used for competitive grants to LEAs to fund the recruitment, training and employment of drug and school safety program coordinators at those schools with the worst drug, discipline, and violence problems.

A 1997 evaluation of programs implemented with SDFSCA funds found that some drug abuse programs improved student outcome, but effects were generally small - few schools employed program approaches found effective in previous research and program delivery was inconsistent. In response, ED has proposed steps to strengthen the effectiveness of prevention education programs.

# INTRODUCTION

The Safe and Drug-Free Schools and Communities Act (SDFSCA), administered by the Department of Education (ED), funds both grants to the

## The Safe and Drug-Free Schools and Communities Program

states and national programs to support substance abuse education and violence prevention activities. The Safe and Drug-Free Schools and Communities (SDFSC) program is funded at $566 million for FY 1999, $10 million more than the FY 1998 appropriations (P.L. 105-78, H.R. 2264). The bulk of program funds, $441 million, are designated for state grants; national programs receive $90 million and a new Coordinator Initiative will receive $35 million. The $90 million under the national programs will support community-wide approaches to creating safe and drug-free schools. Coordinator Initiative funds will be used for competitive grants to local educational agencies (LEAs) to fund the recruitment, training and employment of drug and school safety program coordinators at those schools with the worst drug, discipline, and violence problems. Additionally, the SDFSC program appropriations include $40 million to improve children's mental health services under the Substance Abuse and Mental Health Services Administration (SAMHSA) in the Department of Health and Human Services (HHS), for a total of $165 million for new efforts aimed at drug and violence prevention in schools.

The Drug-Free Schools and Communities Act was established by the 1986 Anti-Drug Abuse Act (P.L. 99-570). It has been amended several times: by the Hawkins/Stafford Elementary and Secondary School Improvement Amendments of 1988 (P.L. 100-297), the 1988 Anti-Drug Abuse Act (P.L.100-690), the Drug-Free Schools and Communities Act Amendments of 1989 (P.L. 101-226), and the Crime Control Act of 1990 (P.L. 101-647). The Improving America's Schools Act of 1994 (P.L. 103-382), reauthorized the Act as the Safe and Drug-Free Schools and Communities Act of 1994, adding violence prevention to the program's original emphasis on substance abuse education. The purpose of the Act, as reauthorized, is "to support programs to meet the seventh National Education Goal by preventing violence in and around schools and by strengthening programs that prevent the illegal use of alcohol, tobacco, and drugs, involve parents, and are coordinated with related federal, state, and community efforts and resources."[1] The program is authorized through FY 1999.

---

[1] Title IV of the Elementary and Secondary Education Act, Section 4003.

## BACKGROUND

### Adolescent Drug Use

Long-term studies of drug use suggest that children most often begin to use drugs (including tobacco and alcohol) at about age 12 or 13. Many researchers have observed young teens moving from the illicit use of legal substances (such as tobacco, alcohol, and inhalants) to the use of illicit drugs. Marijuana is usually the first illicit drug used by teens. Federally supported surveys have shown that teen use of illicit drugs, alcohol, and tobacco has generally increased between 1991 and 1997.

The National Household Survey on Drug Abuse (NHSDA) provides estimates of the prevalence of use of a variety of illicit drugs, alcohol, and tobacco by the noninstitutionalized population age 12 and older. Figure 1 illustrates the decrease in illicit drug use between 1979 and 1992 with subsequent increases from 1992-1997 (with some interim decreases). According to the 1997 NHSDA, 11.4% of youth age 12-17 are current illicit drug users (see Figure 1). The highest rates of illicit drug use for teens were found among those ages 16-17 (19.2%) and ages 18-20 (17.3%).[2]

The Monitoring the Future (MTF) Survey assesses tobacco, alcohol, and illicit drug use by $8^{th}$, $10^{th}$, and $12^{th}$ graders nationwide. The 1998 MTF survey, shows that the use of any illicit drug has decreased for $8^{th}$, $10^{th}$, and $12^{th}$ graders since 1997. The same trend is true for the use of marijuana for all three grade levels, the largest decrease was seen in $10^{th}$ graders.[3]

---

[2] U.S. Dept. of Health and Human Services. Substance Abuse and Mental Health Services Administration. *National Household Survey on Drug Abuse: Preliminary Results, 1997.* August 1998.

[3] U.S. Dept. of Health and Human Services. National Institute on Drug Abuse. *Monitoring the Future, 1998.* December 1998.

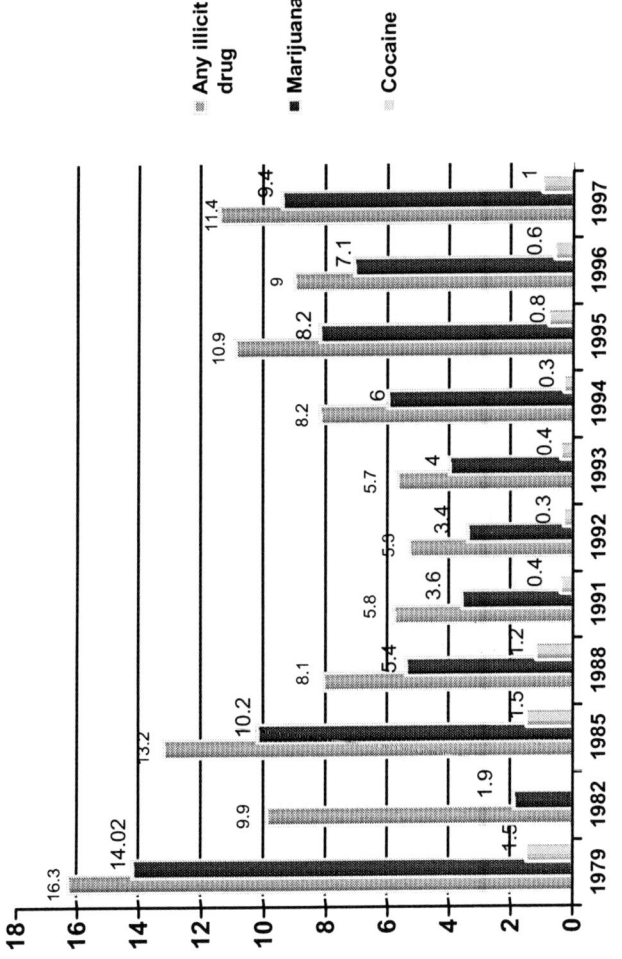

Figure 1. Trends in Past Month Drug Use, Ages 12-17: 1979-1997

Source: DHHS, National Household Survey on Drug Abuse; Preliminary Results, 1997.

According to a recent survey by the National Center for Alcohol and Substance Abuse (CASA) at Columbia University, 35% of teens feel drugs are the most important problem they face. By the time they are age 17, more than half of teens have seen drugs sold on their school grounds, nearly two-thirds report they can buy marijuana within a day, and three-fourths know someone who has used LSD, cocaine, or heroin.[4]

## Violence in Schools

One of the nation's education goals for the year 2000 is to ensure safe schools for all students. In 1994, a violence prevention component was added to the Drug-Free Schools and Communities Act. According to the National Crime Victimization Survey, an estimated 2.7 million violent crimes take place annually either at or near schools. The 1994 Monitoring the Future Survey found that 20% of $8^{th}$, $10^{th}$, and $12^{th}$ graders had been threatened and nearly 10% had been injured by a weapon at school. Other surveys indicate that violence and the threat of violence in schools are on the rise. The 1997 Youth Risk Behavior Survey (YRBS), conducted by the Centers for Disease Control and Prevention (CDC) found that almost one fifth (18.3%) of students had carried a gun, knife, or club on at least one of the 30 days preceding the survey.[5] The Schools and Staffing Survey (SASS), conducting by ED, found an increasing percentage of teachers in public elementary and secondary schools reporting physical conflicts among students and weapons possession as moderate or serious problems in their schools. In the 1987-1988 school year, 26% of teachers in public secondary schools reported physical conflict among students as moderate or serious problems in their schools; the percentage rose to 40% in the 1993-1994 school year. Likewise, in the 1987-1988 school year 11% of public secondary school teachers reported that weapons possession was a moderate or serious problem in their schools, whereas, in the 1993-1994 school year, nearly three times that many (30%) felt it was a problem.[6]

---

[4] Center on Alcohol and Substance Abuse. *Back to School 1997 - The CASA National Survey of American Attitudes on Substance Abuse III: Teens and Their Parents, Teachers and Principals.* September 1997.

[5] U.S. Dept. of Health and Human Services. Centers for Disease Control and Prevention. *Youth Risk Behavior Surveillance - United States, 1997.* Morbidity and Mortality Weekly Report, August 14, 1998

[6] U.S. Dept. of Education. Office of Educational Research and Improvement. *How Safe Are the Public Schools: What Do Teachers Say?* Issue Brief NCES 96-842, April 1996.

Research conducted over the past 20 years in the area of substance abuse prevention has helped to identify important factors that put young people at risk for or protect them from drug use. "Risk" factors and "protective" factors encompass psychological, behavioral, family, and social characteristics. Researchers believe that prevention efforts that focus on family and peer relationships and school and community environments can enhance protective factors and reduce risk factors.[7] Knowledge about these risk and protective factors has allowed intervention researchers to study the effectiveness of various prevention approaches by using rigorous research designs and testing and implementing effective drug abuse prevention interventions in real-world settings.[8] To be most effective, many researchers believe substance abuse prevention education programs should be initiated when children are young. Schools can play an important role in delivering prevention programming. Schools offer the opportunity to reach all young people, and also serve as important settings for specific subpopulations at risk for drug abuse, such as children with behavioral problems or learning disabilities, and those who are potential drop-outs. The Safe and Drug-Free Schools and Communities program, with FY1999 funding level of $566 million, is a key component of the nation's drug use prevention strategy.

## GRANTS TO STATES

**Table 1** shows how FY1998 SDFSC program funds were distributed and how they compare with FY1999 funding.[9] State grant and national program funds under the Act are appropriated separately. Funds appropriated for the state grants are distributed as follows: 1% to the Territories (Guam, American Samoa, the Virgin Islands, and the Commonwealth of the Northern Mariana Islands); 1% to the Secretary of the Interior to carry out programs for Indian youth; 0.2% for programs for Native Hawaiians; and

---

[7] Reducing risk factors focuses on trying to lessen the negative effect of factors that impinge on one's life that have been shown or theorized to relate to drug and alcohol use. These factors include: availability of drugs and alcohol, community laws and norms favorable to drug and alcohol use, extreme economic deprivation, family conflict, family history of problems with use, favorable parental attitudes and involvement in problem use, early and persistent antisocial behavior, academic failure, alienation and rebellion, and friends who engage in problem behavior. Enhancement of protective factors focuses on increasing an individual's resilience in dealing with potentially high-risk situations (such as dysfunctional families, schools, and communities).

[8] U.S. Dept. of Health and Human Services. National Institute of Drug Abuse. *Preventing Drug Use Among Children and Adolescents: A Research-Based Guide.* March 1997.

$1,000,000 for a national Impact evaluation. The remainder is distributed to the states, the District of Columbia, and the Commonwealth of Puerto Rico, Half on the basis of school-aged population and half on the basis of grants under Part A of Chapter I of Title I of the Elementary and Secondary Education Act (ESEA) as amended. No state receives less than 0.5% of the amount allotted to all the states. The state and local educational agencies of each state receive 80% of the state's grant under the program for drug and violence prevention activities, the Office of the Governor receives 20%.

## Allocations to State Education Agencies

The state grants program is forward-funded, meaning that grants used to fund programs during the 1999-2000 school year are part of the FY1999 appropriation and will be distributed to use states during the summer of 1999. A SEAs application for SDFSC funds must include such information as the prevalence of drug use and violence by youth in the state's schools and communities, the state's measurable goals and objectives for drug and violence prevention, and a description of how the state's progress toward meeting these goals will be assessed. States are required to report their progress to the Secretary of ED every 3 years. Of the funds allocated to each SEA, 5% may be used by the agency for training and technical assistance in drug and violence prevention and to address violence associated with prejudice and intolerance; curricular materials; programs for Local Education Agencies (LEAs) and demonstration projects in drug and violence prevention; assistance to economically disadvantaged or sparsely populated areas; and evaluation activities. Up to 4% of the SEA grant may be used for administration. A SEA must distribute at least 91% of its allocation to LEAs; 70% to LEAs based on the relative enrollments in public and private nonprofit elementary and secondary schools within the boundaries of such agencies, 30% to LEAs that the SEA determines have the greatest need for additional funds to carry out drug and violence prevention programs. Where appropriate and consistent with a state's need assessment, not less than 25% of this amount is distributed to LEAs located in rural and urban areas; such sums may be distributed to up to 10% of the LEAs in the state of five such agencies, whichever is greater.

In determining which LEAs have the greatest need for additional funds, the SEA considers data for LEAs in such areas as rates of youth alcohol or

---

[9] Table 1 is based on information provided by the Department of Education and use of the Formula for the Program.

drug use; victimization of youth by violence and crime; arrests and convictions of youth for violent or substance abuse-related crime; extent of illegal gang activity; violence associated with prejudice and intolerance; referrals of youth to substance abuse treatment and rehabilitation programs, or to juvenile court; and reported cases of child abuse and domestic violence.

LEAs are required to submit to their SEA applications for funding. These applications, developed in consultation with community-based local or regional advisory councils, must include as assessment of the substance abuse and violence problems of students in the community, a description of how the LEA's substance abuse and violence prevention plan is consistent with that of the state, and descriptions of the LEA's prevention goals and how progress toward them will be measured. An LEA uses SDFSCA funds to adopt and carry out a comprehensive drug and violence prevention program designed to prevent the use, possession, and distribution of tobacco, alcohol, and illegal drugs by students, and the illegal use, possession, and distribution of such substances by employees. Such a program would also prevent violence, promote school safety, and create a disciplined environment conducive to learning. The program would promote the involvement of parents and coordination with community groups and agencies. A comprehensive drug and violence prevention program may include:

- drug prevention and education programs that address the consequences of the use of illegal drugs, promote a sense of individual responsibility, and provide information about effective techniques for resisting peer pressure to use illegal drugs;
- drug prevention programs which emphasize students' sense of individual responsibility;
- drug prevention and education programs that address the consequences of violent and disruptive behavior, sexual harassment and abuse, and victimization associated with prejudice and intolerance.
- violence prevention programs for school-aged youth which emphasize student's sense of individual responsibility;
- professional development for teachers and other staff;
- before- and after-school programs; (7) Drug Abuse Resistance Education (DARE) programs, including classroom instruction by uniformed law enforcement officers; and
- evaluation of such activities.

Table 1. Allocation of Funds, FY1998 and FY1999

| Expenditure category | Amount (FY1998 appropriations) | Percent share of total for FY1998 | Amount (FY1999 appropriations) | Percent share of total for FY1999 |
|---|---|---|---|---|
| Total | $556,000,000 | 100% | $566,000,000 | 100.00% |
| National programs | $25,000,000 | 4.5% | $90,000,000 | 15.9% |
| Coordinator initiative | $- | 0.0% | $35,000,000 | 6.2% |
| State grants program | $531,000,000 | 95.5% | $441,000,000 | 77.9% |
| State grant program | | Percent share of state grants total (FY1998) | | Percent share of state grants total (FY1998) |
| Set-aside for territories (1% of state grants) | $5,310,000 | 1.0% | $4,410,000 | 1.0% |
| Set-aside for programs for Indian youth (1% of state grants) | $5,310,000 | 1.0% | $4,410,000 | 1.0% |
| Set-aside for programs for Native Hawaiians (0.2% of state grants) | $1,062,000 | 0.2% | $882,000 | 0.2% |
| Set-aside for evaluations | $1,000,000 | 0.2% | $1,000,000 | 0.2% |
| State grants to governors and state educational agencies (SEAs) | $518,318,000 | 97.6% | $430,298,000 | 97.6% |

| Expenditure category | Amount (FY1998 appropriations) | Percent share of total for FY1998 | Amount (FY1999 appropriations) | Percent share of total for FY1999 |
|---|---|---|---|---|
| Governors share of state programs | | Percent share of governors and SEAs total (FY1998) | | Percent share of governors and SEAs total (FY1999) |
| Amounts to governors (20% of grants to governors and SEAs) | $103,663,000 | 20.0% | $86,941,600 | 20.2% |
| Minimum share to law enforcement education partnerships (10% of governors share) | $10,366,000 | 2.0% | $8,694,160 | 2.0% |
| Maximum share for administration (5% of governors share) | $5,183,150 | 1.0% | $4,347,080 | 1.0% |
| State educational agencies (SEAs) share of state funds | | Percent share of state grants total (FY1998) | | Percent share of state grants total (FY1999) |
| Amounts to SEAs (80% of grants to governors and SEAs) | $414,654,400 | 78.1% | $347,766,400 | 78.9% |
| Maximum share to be used by SEAs for program activities (5% of SEA share) | $20,732,720 | 3.9% | $17,388,320 | 3.9% |

| Expenditure category | Amount (FY1998 appropriations) | Percent share of total for FY1998 | Amount (FY1999 appropriations) | Percent share of total for FY1999 |
|---|---|---|---|---|
| Maximum share for SEA administration (4% of funds reserved for SEAs) | $16,586,176 | 3.1% | $13,910,656 | 3.2% |
| Local education agencies (LEAs) share of state funds | | Percent share of state grants total (FY1998) | | Percent share of state grants total (FY1999) |
| Minimum share to be allocated to LEAs (91% of the SEA share) | $377,335,504 | 71.1% | $316,467,424 | 71.8% |
| Portion allocated to high-need areas (30% of LEA share) | $113,200,651 | 21.3% | $94,940,227 | 21.5% |
| Portion allocated on enrollments (70% of LEA share) | $264,134,853 | 49.7% | $221,527,197 | 50.2% |

**Source:** Produced with information by the Department of Education.

An LEA may spend 20% of its SDFSCA funds for the support of "safe zones of passage" for students between home and school, and for the acquisition and installation of mental detectors and hiring of security personnel, but only if it has not received any other federal funding for such activities.

The FY1999 appropriation earmarks $125 million of state grants funding for competitive grants to school districts based on the severity of their schools' drug or safety programs and the quality of their proposed prevention activities. The Department of Education believes this earmark will allow them to target considerable funding to a limited number of high-need districts, while at the same time providing an incentive for districts to implement the most effective prevention strategies.[10] These funds will be targeted directly to the local, not the state, level.

## Allocations to Governors

The funds allocated to the Office of the Governor are used for grants to or contracts with parent and community groups and organizations, and other public and private nonprofit entities for local drug and violence prevention activities, Priority is to be given to programs and activities that serve children and youth who are not normally served by state or LEAs, or populations that need special services or additional resources (such as preschoolers, youth in juvenile detention facilities, runaway or homeless children and youth, pregnant and parenting teenagers, and school dropouts).

In general, grants and contracts are used for such programs and activities as:

- disseminating information about drug and violence prevention;
- training parents, law enforcement and judicial officials, social and health service providers, and community leaders;
- developing and implementing community-based programs that link community resources with schools and integrated services;
- planning and implementing activities that coordinate the efforts of state agencies with efforts of the SEA and its LEAs;
- activities to protect students traveling to and from school;
- before- and after-school programs that encourage drug- and violence-free lifestyles;

---

[10] *Ibid.*

- activities that promote the awareness of and sensitivity to alternatives to violence;
- developing and implementing strategies to prevent and reduce violence associated with prejudice and intolerance;
- developing and implementing strategies to prevent illegal activity;
- coordinating and conducting community-wide violence and safety assessments and surveys;
- service-learning projects that encourage drug- and violence-free lifestyles; and
- evaluating such programs and activities.

At least 10% of the amount allocated to the Office of the Governor is to be used for grants to law enforcement agencies (including district attorneys) in consortium with LEAs or community-based agencies for law enforcement education partnerships. These partnerships carry out such drug abuse and violence prevention activities as:

- Project DARE[11] and other programs that provide classroom instruction by uniformed law enforcement officials;
- Project Legal Lives and other programs in which district attorneys provide classroom instruction in the law and legal system which emphasizes interactive learning techniques, such as mock trial competitions;
- partnerships between law enforcement and child guidance professionals; and
- before- and after-school activities.

Not more than 5% of the Governor's allocation may be used for administrative costs.

According to the ED, the SDFSC state grants program serves more than 40 million students in over 97% of the nation's school districts. The Department estimates average per-pupil spending of $7.91 in FY1997. **Table 2** shows FY1999 state grants allocated by state.

---

[11] See CRS Report 95-740, *Drug Abuse Resistance Education (DARE)*, by Jennifer A.Neisner.

Table 2. Safe and Drug-Free Schools and Communities State Grants Allocation, FY1999

| State | Total allotment (100%) | Allotment to SEA (80%) | Allotment to governor (20%) |
|---|---|---|---|
| US TOTAL | $430,298,000 | $344,238,400 | $86,059,600 |
| Alabama | 6,790,339 | 5,432,271 | 1,358,068 |
| Alaska | 2,151,490 | 1,721,192 | 430,298 |
| Arizona | 6,947,528 | 5,558,022 | 1,389,506 |
| Arkansas | 4,145,468 | 3,316,374 | 829,094 |
| California | 49,465,650 | 39,572,520 | 9,893,130 |
| Colorado | 5,043,675 | 4,034,940 | 1,008,735 |
| Connecticut | 4,312,955 | 3,450,364 | 862,591 |
| Delaware | 2,151,490 | 1,721,192 | 430,298 |
| Florida | 19,869,610 | 15,895,688 | 3,973,922 |
| Georgia | 11,398,716 | 9,118,973 | 2,279,743 |
| Hawaii | 2,151,490 | 1,721,192 | 430,298 |
| Idaho | 2,151,490 | 1,721,192 | 430,298 |
| Illinois | 18,593,672 | 14,874,938 | 3,718,734 |
| Indiana | 7,723,005 | 6,178,404 | 1,544,601 |
| Iowa | 3,699,409 | 2,959,527 | 739,882 |
| Kansas | 3,648,276 | 2,918,621 | 729,655 |
| Kentucky | 6,528,503 | 5,222,802 | 1,305,701 |
| Louisiana | 9,061,639 | 7,249,311 | 1,812,328 |
| Maine | 2,151,490 | 1,721,192 | 430,298 |
| Maryland | 6,601,567 | 5,281,254 | 1,320,313 |

| State | Total allotment (100%) | Allotment to SEA (80%) | Allotment to governor (20%) |
|---|---|---|---|
| Massachusetts | 8,469,847 | 6,775,878 | 1,693,969 |
| Michigan | 16,910,263 | 13,528,210 | 3,382,053 |
| Minnesota | 6,298,795 | 5,039,036 | 1,259,759 |
| Mississippi | 5,822,877 | 4,658,302 | 1,164,575 |
| Missouri | 7,852,625 | 6,282,100 | 1,570,525 |
| Montana | 2,151,490 | 1,721,192 | 430,298 |
| Nebraska | 2,258,476 | 1,806,781 | 451,695 |
| Nevada | 2,151,490 | 1,721,192 | 430,298 |
| New Hampshire | 2,151,490 | 1,721,192 | 430,298 |
| New Jersey | 10,457,911 | 8,366,329 | 2,091,582 |
| New Mexico | 3,281,003 | 2,624,802 | 656,201 |
| New York | 32,689,730 | 26,151,784 | 6,537,946 |
| North Carolina | 9,522,219 | 7,617,775 | 1,904,444 |
| North Dakota | 2,151,490 | 1,721,192 | 430,298 |
| Ohio | 17,112,538 | 13,690,030 | 3,422,508 |
| Oklahoma | 5,149,345 | 4,119,476 | 1,029,869 |
| Oregon | 4,394,500 | 3,515,600 | 878,900 |
| Pennsylvania | 18,159,544 | 14,527,635 | 3,631,909 |
| Rhode Island | 2,151,490 | 1,721,192 | 430,298 |
| South Carolina | 5,560,162 | 4,448,130 | 1,112,032 |
| South Dakota | 2,151,490 | 1,721,192 | 430,298 |
| Tennessee | 7,607,750 | 6,086,200 | 1,521,550 |
| Texas | 34,278,436 | 27,422,749 | 6,855,687 |

| State | Total allotment (100%) | Allotment to SEA (80%) | Allotment to governor (20%) |
|---|---|---|---|
| Utah | 2,956,532 | 2,365,226 | 591,306 |
| Vermont | 2,151,490 | 1,721,192 | 430,298 |
| Virginia | 8,022,627 | 6,418,102 | 1,604,525 |
| Washington | 7,466,311 | 5,973,049 | 1,493,262 |
| West Virginia | 3,359,970 | 2,687,976 | 671,994 |
| Wisconsin | 7,715,408 | 6,172,326 | 1,543,082 |
| Wyoming | 2,151,490 | 1,721,192 | 430,298 |
| District of Columbia | 2,141,490 | 1,721,192 | 430,298 |
| Puerto Rico | 11,000,259 | 8,800,207 | 2,200,052 |
| Total for outlying areas: | 4,410,000 | 3,528,000 | $430,298,000 |
| American Samoa | 757,081 | 605,665 | 151,416 |
| Guam | 1,766,299 | 1,413,039 | 353,260 |
| Northern Mariana Islands | 431,396 | 345,117 | 86,279 |
| Republic of Palau | 0 | 0 | 0 |
| Virgin Islands | 1,455,224 | 1,164,179 | 291,045 |
| Total for mandatory set-asides | 6,292,000 | N/A | N/A |
| Indian youth set-aside | 4,410,000 | N/A | N/A |
| Native Hawaiian set-aside | 882,000 | N/A | N/A |
| Evaluation set-aside | 1,000,000 | N/A | N/A |
| Total funding | 441,000,000 | 347,766,400 | 86,941,600 |

**Source:** U.S. Department of Education.

## NATIONAL PROGRAMS

National programs under the SDFSCA provide funds for a variety of programs designed of prevent the illegal use of drugs and violence among students at all educational levels. The national authority, as amended by P.L. 103-382, replaces previous authority for grants to institutions of higher education for model demonstrations and postsecondary prevention programs, programs for Indian youths and for Hawaiian natives, regional centers, school personnel training grants, emergency grants, and other discretionary federal activities. The FY1999 appropriation for national programs is $90 million.

National Program funds have been used for such activities as:

- model programs for training school personnel, parents, ad members of the community;
- demonstrations of innovative approaches to drug and violence prevention;
- direct services to school systems with especially severe drug and violence programs;
- financial and technical assistance to institutions of higher education for model drug prevention and campus safety programs;
- grants to LEAs and community-based organizations to provide assistance to localities most directly affected by hate crimes;
- drug and violence program evaluation; and
- other federal initiatives that address unmet national needs relating to the purposes of law, including developing and disseminating model curricula and other drug and violence prevention information and materials.

In 1999, the Department's principles of effectiveness for drug prevention programs include (effective July 1998):[12]

- Grant recipients will base their programs on a thorough assessment of objective data about the drug and violence problems in the schools and communities they serve.

---

[12] U.S. Dept. of Education. FY1999 Annual Plan. Volume 1. Objective Pérformance Plan and Data Quality. February 27, 1998.

- Grant recipients will, with the assistance of community representatives, establish a set of measurable goals and objectives, and design their activities to meet those goals and objectives.
- Grant recipients will design and implement their activities based on research or evaluation that provides evidence that the strategies used prevent or reduce drug use, violence, or disruptive behavior.
- Grant recipients will evaluate their programs periodically to access their progress toward achieving their goals and objectives and use their evaluation results to refine, improve, and strengthen their program and to refine their goals and objective as appropriate.

For further information on the efforts of institutions of higher education to address alcohol and other drug problems, see the World Wide Web site of the Department of Education's Higher Education Center for Alcohol and Other Drug Prevention at [http://www.edc.org/hec/index.html].

## PROGRAM FUNDING

Since 1987, the Safe and Drug-Free Schools Program has received nearly $6.2 billion. As Table 3 indicates, appropriations for the program increased significantly during its early history before declining in the period 1993-1998. Continued support for the program was uncertain for fiscal years 1995 and 1996. In both years, however, funding levels ultimately remained fairly constant compared to FY1994 funding.

The FY1997 appropriation of $556 million was an increase of nearly 20% ($90 million) over the FY1996 funding level. The Congress provided level funding for the program for FY1998, $556 million ($531 million for state grants and $25 million for national programs) (P.L. 105-78). The FY1999 budget is $566 million ($411 for state grants, $90 million for national programs, and $35 million for the Coordinator Initiative).

**Table 3. Safe and Drug-Free Schools and Communities Act Appropriations, FY1987-FY1999 (dollars in thousands)**

| Fiscal year | Grants to states | Other | Total |
|---|---|---|---|
| 1987 | $161,046 | $38,954 | $200,000 |
| 1988 | 191,480 | 38,296 | 229,776 |
| 1989 | 287,730 | 66,770 | 354,500 |
| 1990 | 437,881 | 101,319 | 539,200 |
| 1991 | 497,709 | 95,591 | 539,300 |
| 1992 | 507,663 | 116,300 | 623,963 |
| 1993 | 498,565 | 99,802 | 598,367 |
| 1994 | 369,500 | 117,662 | 487,162 |
| 1995 | 440,981 | 25,000 | 465,981[b] |
| 1996 | 440,978 | 24,993 | 465,971 |
| 1997 | 530,978 | 25,000[c] | 555,987 |
| 1998 | 531,000 | 25,000 | 556,000 |
| 1999 | $441,000 | $125,000[d] | $566,000 |

[a] Until FY1995, included personnel training, national programs, and emergency grants; for FY1995 onward, includes national programs only.
[b] Amount reflects rescission of $15.981 million from the FY1995 appropriation.
[c] Reflects reprogramming of $25 million appropriated for state grants to national programs.
[d] includes $90 million for national programs and $35 million for the Coordinator Initiative.

# EVALUATION OF THE DRUG-FREE SCHOOLS PROGRAM

There have been substantial concerns about the effectiveness of some drug prevention programs currently being implemented in schools with federal funds. Research on the effectiveness of school-based prevention programs conducted soon after the Drug-Free Schools and Communities program was authorized was inconclusive. While some programs demonstrated short-term success in improving students' awareness of the dangerous consequences of illicit drug use, these programs often had little apparent long-term impact on student behavior on drug use. The Office of Technology Assessment (OTA), in a 1991 report on adolescent health,[13]

---

[13] U.S. Congress. Office of Technology Assessment. *Adolescent Health - Volume II: Background and the Effectiveness of Selected Prevention and Treatment Services.* OTA-H-466, November 1991. Washington, GPO, 1991. P.II-544.

concluded from a review of efforts to prevent or delay the onset of adolescent illicit drug use that most prevention programs targeted at individuals "have yet failed to make a compelling case for their effectiveness". Some models, according to OTA, "show some positive effects in delaying increases in drug use, but the effects are generally small. Whether these models are of much practical significance in reducing drug use among adolescents is debatable." The OTA report, however, also concluded that some substance abuse prevention programs that produce little change in adolescents' use of alcohol and drugs, may be effective in other important respects, such as enhancing general life skills in such areas as social competence and decision making, and increasing knowledge about a range of psychoactive substances and possible physiological and developmental effects. The General Accounting Office (GAO) in a 1990 survey on school-based programs[14] concluded that, while evaluations of such programs generally have lacked needed scientific rigor and as a result offer little information on what works, "the message of drug and alcohol dangers is reaching the children". In the opinion of both students and principals, according to GAO's discussions in 18 schools, drug and alcohol abuse among school-age children would be worse without the federally funded program.

In February 1997, the Department of Education released the summary of its longitudinal study investigating the effectiveness of school-based prevention programs in school districts receiving DFSCA funds.[15] This study, conducted by the Research Triangle Institute (RTI), echoed some of the findings of previous research. Researchers found that drug prevention programs improved student outcomes, but that effects were generally small. Researchers collected data from some 10,000 students in 19 school districts over 4 years, and found that prevention programs varied greatly both among and within school districts.[16] The authors note that drug education experts believe inconsistent or incomplete delivery of the prevention curriculum is one of the main reasons approaches that proved effective under test conditions may not show positive results when implemented elsewhere.

---

[14] U.S. Congress. General Accounting Office. *Drug Education: School-Based Programs Seen as Useful but Impact Unknown*. GAO/HRD-91-27, November 1990. Washington, GPO, 1990.
[15] Silvia, E. Suyapa and Judy Thorne. *School-Based Drug Prevention Programs: A Longitudinal Study in Selected School Districts*. Executive Summary. Research Triangle Institute, prepared under contract for the U.S. Department of Education. February 1997. Research Triangle Park, NC.
[16] The data collected for this study predates the implementation of changes made by the Improving America's Schools Act of 1994 (P.L. 103-382), which among other things added a violence prevention component.

Students in districts where prevention programs had greater stability over time and more extensive program components had somewhat better outcomes than students in districts where fewer program components were offered. RTI found that few districts employed prevention approaches that have been found effective in previous research, while approaches that have not shown evidence of effectiveness or have not been evaluated properly were the most commonly used. The study also showed that the use of drugs was related to violent behavior in schools, with a larger percentage of current users of alcohol and drugs initiating school fights than non-users, and those schools reporting higher levels of gang activity and violence also reporting greater drug use and more tolerant views toward drugs. In light of their findings, RTI concluded that district programs need to be stable and extensive, providing both prevention-related classroom instruction and school-wide special events.

In response to these findings, in June, 1998, ED promulgated its "principles of effectiveness." These principles are designs to improve the accountability of the program by requiring all Safe and Drug-Free Schools projects to include an assessment of school districts' needs, to establish measurable goals and objectives, to be based on research or evaluation evidence of what works, and to be evaluated periodically to assess program effectiveness. Districts will be expected to use the results of these evaluations to improve their programs.

In October 1997, GAO released a study specific to the Safe and Drug-Free Schools program.[17] The study found that the Safe and Drug-Free Schools program is one of 70 substance- and violence-prevention programs funded by the federal government. The study concludes that the lack of uniform information on program activities and effectiveness may create a problem for federal oversight.

For further information on the Safe and Drug-Free Schools and Communities programs, see the SDFSC World Wide Web site at [http://www.ed.gov.offices.OESE/SDFS/index.html].

---

[17] U.S. Congress. General Accounting Office. *Safe and Drug-Free Schools-Balancing Accountability with State and Local Flexibility.* GAO/HEHS-98-3, October 1997. Washington, GPO, 1997.

*Chapter 4*

# THE SAFE AND DRUG-FREE SCHOOLS AND COMMUNITIES PROGRAM: BACKGROUND AND CONTEXT

## Edith Fairman Cooper

### SUMMARY

The No Child Left Behind Act (P.L 107-110), amends and reauthorizes the Safe and Drug-Free Schools and Communities Act (SDFSCA) as Part A of Title IV - 21$^{st}$ Century Schools. The Development of Education administers SDFSCA through the Safe and Drug Schools and Communities program, which is the federal government's major initiative to prevent drug abuse and violence in and around schools. Through the Act, state grants are awarded by formula to outlying areas, state educational agencies, and local educational agencies in all 50 states, the District of Columbia (DC) and the Commonwealth of Puerto Rico. Also, funds go to a state's Chief Executive Officer (Governor) for creating programs to deter youth from using drugs and committing violent acts in schools. National programs are supported through discretionary funds for a variety of national leadership projects designed to prevent drug abuse and violence among all educational levels, from preschool through the postsecondary level.

There are other federally sponsored substance abuse and violence prevention programs administered in the Departments of Justice, Health and

Human Services, and other agencies. Those programs are not discussed in this report.

Despite the reports about violence in the nation's schools and the surge in multiple homicides in schools in recent years, the *2000 Annual Report on School Safety* indicates that the nation's schools are generally considered to be safe. Also, researchers found that reports of the presence of street gangs on school property, which can cause students to feel less safe, have declined. Although crimes were still occurring in schools, some students seemed to feel more secure at school now than they did a few years ago, while many others seemed to feel safe. Such feelings, the report reveals, depend on the racial and/or ethnic group of the students. Larger percentages of African American and Latino students feared attack or harm at school than white students. At the same time, according to the U.S. Secret Service in its *Safe School Initiative* report, in more than three-fourths of the school shooting cases, the attackers were white.

The Monitoring the Future study conducted by the University of Michigan revealed mixed results concerning drug use among the students. Cigarette use declined from 2000 to 2001 among $8^{th}$, $10^{th}$, and $12^{th}$ graders. The use of MDMA (ecstasy), which had increased in the past few years, slowed from 2000 to 2001 among students in all grade levels surveyed. Similarly, heroin use decreased significantly among $10^{th}$ and $12^{th}$ graders, and a gradual decline in the use of inhalants continued in 2001, most notably among $12^{th}$ graders. All other illicit drug use remained stable from 2000 to 2001. Long-term available trends for illicit drug use in $12^{th}$ graders, showed that current levels of illicit drug use were far below the 27-year peaks that occurred in the 1970s and early 1980s.

## INTRODUCTION

Since 1986, drug abuse of students in school has been a congressional concern. In 1994, this concern was expanded to include violence occurring in and around schools. A U.S. General Accounting Office (GAO) report stated that in 1994, when the Safe and Drug-Free Schools and Communities Act was enacted, about 3 million violent crimes and thefts occurred annually in or near schools, which equaled almost 16,000 incidents per school day.[1] The Schools and Staffing Survey (SASS) conducted by the National Center for Education Statistics (NCES) indicated that in the 1993-94 school year, violence in public schools was on the rise and schools appeared less safe than in the 1987-88 school year. From the 1987-88 school year to the 1993-94 school year, an increasing percentage of public elementary and secondary school teachers reported that physical conflict and weapon possession among students were moderate to serious problems in schools.[2] Similarly, between 1992 and 1995, drug use rates among school-aged youth increased for over 10 different drugs, particularly marijuana, after declining in the 1980s.[3]

To address those concerns, on October 20, 1994, President Clinton signed into law the Improving America's Schools Act (P.L. 103-382), which reauthorized the Elementary and Secondary Education Act (ESEA), and created the Safe and Drug-Free Schools Act (SDFSCA) as Title IV. The 1994 legislation extended, amended, and renamed the Drug-Free Schools and Communities Act of 1988 (P.L. 100-297, DFSCA).[4] Violence prevention was added to the DFSCA's original drug prevention purpose by incorporating the Safe Schools Act.[5] Consequently, the SDFSCA was intended to help deter violence and promote school safety as well as discourage drug use in and around the nation's schools. Funding was authorized for federal, state, and local programs to assist schools in providing a disciplined learning environment free of violence and drug use, including alcohol and tobacco.[6]

On January 8, 2002, the President signed H.R. 1, the No Child Left Behind Act, into law (P.L. 107-110), which reauthorizes SDFSCA within ESEA as Part A of Title IV - 21th Century Schools. The Safe and Drug-Free Schools and Communities Act is administered by the Department of Education (ED. Grants are awarded to states and at the national level for programs to promote school safety and assist in preventing drug abuse. For FY2002, $746.8 million was appropriated for the program. For FY2003, the George W. Bush Administration has requested $644.3 million in funding for SDFSC program.

---

[1] U.S. General Accounting Office, *Safe and Drug-Free Schools: Balancing Accountability With State and Local Flexibility,* GAO report GAO/HEHS-98-3 (Washington: October 1997), p.1.
[2] U.S. Department of Education, Office of Educational Research and Improvement, National Center for Education Statistics, "How Safe Are the Public Schools: What Do Teachers Say?" *Issue Brief,* NCES 96-842, April 1996, p. 1.
[3] *Ibid.*
[4] The DSFSCA was originally created by Title IV, Subtitle B of the Anti-Drug Abuse Act of 1986, P.L. 99-570.
[5] The Safe Schools Act was originally created by Title VII of The Goals 2000: Educate America Act of 1994 (P.L. 103-227).
[6] "Title IV - Safe Schools," 1994 *CQ Almanac,* v. 50 (Washington: Congressional Quarterly, Inc., 1994), p. 394.

Although the SDFSC program is the primary federal government program targeted to reduce drug use and violence through educational and prevention methods in the nation's schools,[7] it is one of several substance abuse and violence prevention programs funded by the federal government.[8] In its 1997 report, GAO identified 70 federal programs authorized to provide services for either substance abuse prevention or violence prevention. ED, the Department of Health and Human Services (HHS), and the Department of Justice (DOJ) administered 48 of the programs.[9]

This report discusses various aspects of the SDFSCA as it exists under current law, as newly amended. It begins with background information about the school safety and drug abuse issues, provides a detailed overview of the program, and discusses an evaluation of the SDFSC program.

## SCHOOL SAFETY

The nation's schools are generally considered to be safe, despite the reports about violence and the surge in multiple homicides in schools. The *2002 Annual Report on School Safety (Annual Report)*, published by the Departments of Education and Justice, indicates that school crime[10] rates actually declined between 1992 and 1998. Furthermore, the report qualifies the safety of most schools by stating that, ... "notwithstanding the disturbing reports of violence in our schools, they are becoming even safer."[11] The Office of Juvenile Justice and Delinquency Prevention (OJJDP) study, *Juvenile Offenders and Victims: 1999 National Report*, states that juveniles are at the highest risk of becoming victims of violence at the end of the school day.[12] In addition, *Annual Report* researchers found that reports of the presence of street gangs on school property, which can cause students to feel

---

[7] "About Safe and Drug-Free Schools Program," [http://www.ed.gov/offices/OESE/SDFS/aboutsdf.html], visited February 08, 2002.

[8] U.S. General Accounting Office, *Safe and Drug-Free Schools*, p.8.

[9] U.S. General Accounting Office, *Substance Abuse and Violence Prevention: Multiple Youth Programs Raise Questions of Efficiency and Effectiveness*, GAO testimony before the House Committee on Education and the Workforce, Subcommittee on Oversight and Investigations, GAO/T-HEHS-97-166 (Washington: June 24, 1997), p.5.

[10] School crimes included serious violent crimes such as homicide, suicide, rape, sexual assault, aggravated assault with or without a weapon, and robbery. Less serious or nonviolent crimes included theft/larceny and vandalism of school property.

[11] U.S. Dept. of Education and the U.S. Dept. of Justice, *2000 Annual Report on School Safety*, [http://www.ed.gov/offices/OESE/SDFS/annrept00.pdf], p. iv.

[12] Howard N/Snyder and Melissa Sickmund., *Juvenile Offenders and Victims: 1999 National Report* (Washington, D.C.: Office of Juvenile Justice and Delinquency Prevention, 1999), p. 34.

safe, have declined. Consequently, although crimes are still occurring in schools, some students seem to feel more secure at school now than they did a few years ago, while many others seem to feel less safe at school. Such feelings, the report reveals, depend on racial and/or ethnic group of the students. In 1995 and in 1999, larger percentages of African American and Latino students feared attack or harm at school than white students.[13] At the same time, the U.S. Secret Service started in its study, *Safe School Initiative: An Intern Report on the Prevention of Targeted Violence in Schools*, that in more than three-fourths of the school shooting cases, the attackers were white.[14]

The companion report to the *Annual Report*, entitled *Indicators of School Crime and Safety 2001 (Indicators Study)*, found a mixed picture for school safety. Overall crime rates in schools have decreased, but violence, gangs, and drugs remain evident in some schools, which indicated, the report started, that more work needs to be done.[15] The *Indicatory Study* data were drawn from a variety of independent sources including federal departments and agencies such as the Bureau of Justice Statistics, the National Center for Education Statistics, and the Centers for Disease Control and Prevention. With multiple and independent data sources combined, the authors of the *Indicators Study* hoped to present a more valid picture of school crime and safety. Key findings of the report were as follows:[16]

- From July 1, 1998 to June 30, 1999, 47 school-related violent deaths occurred in the nation's schools - 38 were homicides, 6 were suicides, two were killed by a law enforcement officer in the line of duty, and one was unintentional. Thirty-three of the 38 homicides were school-aged children. A total of 2,407 homicides occurred between July 1, 1998, to June 30, 1999, of children ages 5 to 19 years. Of that total, 2,374 murders occurred away from school, while 33 murders and 4 suicides, out of a grand total of 1,854 in 1999, occurred at school. Of the 6 suicides occurring between July 1, 1998 and June 30, 1999, mentioned above, four were of school-aged children;

---

[13] *2000 Annual Report on School Safety*, p.7.
[14] U.S. Dept. of the Treasury, U.S. Secret Service, National Threat Assessment Center in Collaboration with the U.S. Dept. of education with support from the National Institute of Justice, *Safe School Initiative: An Interim Report on the Prevention of Targeted Violence in Schools*, October 2000, p.5.
[15] P.Kaufman, et al., *Indicators of School Crime and Safety, 2001*, U.S. Depts. Of Education and justice. NCES 2002-113/NCJ-190075 (Washington: 2001), p. iv.
[16] *Ibid.*, pp. v, viii-ix, 2, 4.

- In 1999, 12-to 18-year-old students were victims of over 2.5 million crimes at school, a slight decline from 1998 data. They were, however, more than two times as likely to be victims of nonfatal serious violent crime away from school than at school, with 476,000 serious violent crimes perpetrated on such students away from school compared with 186,000 such incidents at school. The victimization rate for such crimes at school and away from school generally declined from 1992 to 1999.

- In the 1996-97 school year, one serious violent crime was reported to the police or law enforcement representative by 10% of all public schools; 47% of public schools reported a less serious violent or nonviolent crime; and 43% of such schools did not report any such crimes to the police;

- From 1995 to 1999, teachers were victims of 1,708,000 nonfatal crimes at school. This number includes 1,073,000 thefts and 635,000 violent crimes. Those data translate into 79 crimes per 1,000 teachers per year; and

- Between 1995 and 1999, the percentages of students ages 12 to 18 who reported feeling unsafe at school decreased from 9% to 5%. Similarly, during the same time period, the percentage of such students who feared that they would to attacked while going to and from school declined from 7% to 4%.

## School Homicides

The *2000 Annual Report on School Safety* acknowledges that although homicides at school remain extremely rare events, they do occur and affect the perspective of all citizens, particularly children.[17] Research reported by the *Journal of the American Medical Association (JAMA)* discovered that less than 1% of homicides and suicides among school-aged youth occur on school property or when traveling to or from school or at school-sponsored events.[18]

---

[17] *2000 Annual Report on School Safety*, p. 9.
[18] Nancy D.Brener, Thomas R.Simon, Etienne G.Krug, and Richard Lowry, "Recent Trends in Violence-Related Behaviors Among High School Students in the United States," *JAMA*, vol. 285, no.5, August 4, 1999, p.440.

## The1996 Study on School-Related Violent Deaths

In 1996, *JAMA* published the first study investigating violent school-related deaths nationwide that was conducted by researching from the Centers for Disease Control and Prevention (CDC) of the Department of Health and Human Services, the Safe and Drug-Free Schools and Communities Program at ED, the National School Safety Center (NSSC)[19] of Westlake Village, CA, and the National Institute of Justice of DOJ. The period studied covered two consecutive academic years from July 1, 1992, through June 30, 1994 (specifically, July 1, 1992-June 30, 1993 and July 1, 1993-June 30, 1994). Over the two-year period, 105 school-related deaths were identified. The researchers used a case definition for school-associated deaths as "any homicide or suicide in which the fatal injury occurred on the campus of a functioning elementary or secondary school in the United States, while the victim was on the way to or from regular sessions at such a school, or while the victim was attending or traveling to or from an official school-sponsored event."[20] Deaths of students, non-students, and staff members were included.

Two strategies were used in obtaining the data - deaths identified by study collaborators at the ED and the NSSC through newspaper accounts and informal voluntary reports from state and local educational officers, and a systematic search of two computerized newspaper and broadcast media databases. The first strategy revealed 78 possible cases and the second strategy revealed 160 possible cases. Out of the total 238 probable cases, 52 duplicate cases were identified and eliminated, leaving 186 possible cases. The probable cases were confirmed through various sources.[21] As a result, 81 cases were eliminated because they failed to meet the case definition for various reasons. Consequently, the 105 cases were confirmed.

Researchers discovered the following:

---

[19] The National School Safety Center was formerly a national clearinghouse for school safety program information that was funded by ED and DOJ and housed at Pepperdine University in Malibu, CA. In FY1997, federal funding ended and NSSC became a private, non-profit, independent organization. Although NSSC is not a research-based group, it participated in the 1996 released *JAMA* study on school-associated deaths. Discussed in a telephone conservation with the Associate Director of NSSC on July 31, 2001.
[20] S.Patrick Kachur, et al., "School Associated-Violent Deaths in the United States, 1992 to 1994," *JAMA*, vol. 275, no. 22, June 12, 1996, p. 1729-1730.
[21] At least one local press, law enforcement, or school official familiar with each case was contacted and brief interviews were conducted to determine whether the case definition had been met.

- As mentioned above, less than 1% of all homicides among school-aged children, 5 to 19 years, occur in or around school grounds or on the way to and from school;

- 65% of school-related deaths were students, 11% were teachers or other staff members, and 23% were community members who were killed on school property;

- 83% of school homicide or suicide victims were males;

- 23% of the fatal injuries occurred inside the school building, 36% happened outdoors on school property, and 35% occurred off campus; and

- The deaths included in the study occurred in 25 states across the nation and took place in both primary and secondary schools and communities of all sizes.[22]

## Update of the 1996 Study

The December 5, 2001 issue of *JAMA* contains the results of an update of the 1996 study. Entitled, "School-Associated Violent Deaths in the United States, 1994-1999," the study continues where the 1996 research ended and describes the trends and features of such deaths from July 1, 1994, through June 30, 1999.[23] Using a definition similar to the 1996 study, a school-related death case was defined as "a homicide, suicide, legal intervention[24], or unintentional firearm-related death of a student or non-student in which the fatal injury occurred (1) on the camps of a public or private elementary or secondary school, (2) while the victim was on the way to or from such a school, or (3) while the victim was attending or traveling to or from an official school-sponsored event."[25] Researchers discovered that between 1994 and 1999, there were 220 events that led to 253 school-related deaths. Of the 220 events, there was 172 homicides, 30 suicides, 11 homicide-suicide occurrences, 5 legal intervention deaths, and 2 unintentional firearm-related deaths.

---

[22] Centers for Disease Control and Prevention, "Facts About Violence Among Youth and Violence in Schools," *Media Relations Fact Sheets*, April 21, 1999, [http://www.cdc.gov/od/oc/media/fact/violence.htm].

[23] Mark Anderson, et al., "School-Associated Violent Deaths in the United States, 1994-1999," *JAMA*, v. 286, no. 21, December 5, 2001, p. 2695-2702.

[24] A legal intervention is assumed to mean that a student was short by police. The available information about the study that CRS has at this writing, however, does not define the phrase.

[25] *Ibid.*, [http://jama.ama-assn.org/issues/v286n21/abs/joc11149.html].

Several emerging trends were noted in a CDC press release as follows:

- "School-associated violent deaths represent less than one percent of all homicides and suicides that occur among school-aged children."
- "Troubled teens often give potential signals such as writing a note or a journal entry, or they make a threat. In over half the incidents that were examined, some type of signal was given."
- "While the rate of school-associated violent deaths events has decreased significantly during the study time period, the number of multiple-victim events has increased."
- "More than fifty percent of all school-associated violent death events occurred during transition times during the school day - either at the beginning or end of the day or during lunch-time."
- "Homicide perpetrators were far more likely than homicide victims to have expressed previous suicidal behaviors or had a history of criminal charges; been a gang member; associated with high-risk peers or considered a loner; or used alcohol or drugs on a weekly basis. Among students, homicide perpetrators were twice as likely than homicide victims to have been bullied by peers."
- "The rate of school-associated violent deaths was over twice as high for male students."[26]

Researchers conclude and emphasize that such deaths remain rare events but have occurred often enough to detect patterns and to identify possible risk factors. Therefore, this information might assist schools in responding to the problem.

## *Centers for Disease Control and Prevention 2001 Reported Study*

The CDC, which has been involved in school-associated violent deaths research in collaboration with ED and DOJ (as mentioned above), also collected data to assess whether the risk for such deaths varied during the school year. The case definition for school-associated violent deaths used in this study was the same one that was used in the 1996 study discussed above. Researchers analyzed monthly counts of school-associated homicides and

---

[26] U.S. Dept. of Health and Human Services, "Study Finds School-Associated Violent Deaths Rare, Fewer Events But More Deaths Per Event," *CDC Media Relations, Press Release,* December 4, 2001, [http://www.cdc.gov/od/oc/media/pressrel/r011204.htm].

suicides for seven school terms, from September 1, 1992, to June 30, 1999, that occurred among middle, junior, and senior high school students in the nation. For that 7-year period, 209 school-related violent deaths occurred that involved either a homicide or a suicide of a student. As average of 0.14 school-related homicide incidents occurred each school day, which translated to one homicide every 7 school days. Homicide rates usually were higher near the beginning of the fall and spring semesters, and then declined over the subsequent months. An average of 0.03 suicide incidents occurred each school day, which was one suicide every 31 school days. The overall suicide rates were higher during the spring semester than in the fall semester, but did not vary significantly within semesters.[27]

The CDC researchers believe that these findings could be useful for school personnel in planning and implementing school violence prevention programs. They point out that possible explanations exist regarding why high school-related homicide rates occurred at the beginning of each semester. One suggested explanation is that conflicts that began either before or during the semester or holiday break might have escalated into deadly violence when students returned to school for the start of a new semester. Another suggestion was that the beginning of a new semester represented a time of considerable change and stress for students when they have to adapt to new schedules, teachers, and classmates. Such stressors might contribute to violent behavior. For these reasons, they propose that schools should consider policies and programs that might ease student adjustment during the transitional periods.

The researchers warn that the results of the study should be interpreted with caution because incidents were identified from news media reports. Therefore, any such event that was not reported in the news media would not have been included in the study. Reports of suicides were of particular concern because media coverage of such events might be limited or discouraged. If underreporting of suicides did occur, the report states, "coverage probably did not vary by the time of year and would not account for the higher rate observed during the spring semester."[28]

---

[27] "Temporal Variations in School-Associated Student Homicide and Suicide Events - United States, 1992-1999," *MMWR Weekly*, August 10, 2001, vol.50, no.31, pp.657-660. [http://www.cdc.gov/mmvr/preview/mmwrhtml/mm5031a1.htm]
[28] *Ibid.*

## Multiple Deaths and Injuries

There has been an increase in high-profile multiple-victim school shootings since 1996. Those occurrences might tend to skew the public perception about the safety of children and youth at school. On February 2, 1996, a 14-year-old male student walked into a junior high school algebra class in Moses Lake, WA with a hunting rifle and allegedly killed the teacher, two students, and injured a third student. A little over one year later on February 19, 1997, another multiple shooting occurred in a Bethel, Alaska high school when a 16-year-old male student opened fire with a shotgun killing the principal and a student, and wounded two other students. Those incidents appeared to begin a pattern of several multi-victim attacks at various schools across the nation, from the 1995-96 school year through the 1998-99 school term. Using the 1996 study's case definition for school-related violent deaths (see above), during those academic periods, from various news accounts of the incidents, it appears that about 34 students and teachers were killed at school. Also, a larger number of 75 individuals were wounded in the various incidents. One shooting occurred during the 1999-00 school year when four students were wounded, increasing the local to 79 injured. Two incidents occurred in the 2000-01 academic year, increasing the number to 36 students killed and 103 persons wounded, for a total 139 victims from 1995 through 1999. Multiple homicides in schools appeared to be sporadic during the periods discussed, with the largest number of persons killed and wounded in one incident, during the 1998-99 school session (see **Table 1**).

On April 20, 1999, during the 1998-99 school year, an incident that has been called the worst school shooting tragedy in the nation's history by some commentators, occurred at Columbine High School in Littleton, Colorado. Two male students armed with handguns and rifles shot and killed 12 classmates, a teacher, and wounded 23 others, before killing themselves. This incident stirred much concern and questions about safety in the nation's schools. For the 1998-99 school year, it was reported that, "States and Territories... expelled an estimated 3,523 students for bringing a firearm to school."[29]

On March 5, 2001, during the 2000-01 academic year, in what was described as the worst episode of school violence since the Columbine tragedy, a 15-year-old male student randomly shot and killed two students

---

[29] U.S. Dept. of Education, *Fiscal Year 2003 Justifications of Appropriation Estimates to the Congress,* vol. 1, p. C-115.

and wounded 13 others (including two adults - a security guard and a student teacher) at the Santana High School in Santee, California, a community about 10 miles northeast of downtown San Diego. It was reported that the teenager had been belittled by his freshman classmates.

**Table 1. Multiple School-Related Violent Deaths and Injuries, 1995-96 - 2000-01 (as of July 31, 2001)**

| School year | City/town/state | Number of deaths | Number wounded | Total victims |
|---|---|---|---|---|
| 1995-96 | Moses Lake, WA | 3 | 1 | 4 |
| 1996-97 | Bethel, AK | 2 | 2 | 4 |
| 19997-98 | Pearl, MS | 2 | 7 | 9 |
|  | West Paducah, KY | 3 | 5 | 8 |
|  | Jonesboro, AR | 5 | 10 | 15 |
|  | Pomona, CA | 2 | 1 | 3 |
|  | Springfield, OR | 2[a] | 22 | 24 |
|  | Richmond VA | 0 | 2 | 2 |
| 1998-99 | Littleton, CO | 15 | 23 | 38 |
|  | Conyers, GA | 0 | 6 | 6 |
| 1999-2000 | Fort Gibson, OK | 0 | 4 | 4 |
| 2000-20001 | Santee, CA | 2 | 13 | 15 |
|  | Cajon, CA | 0 | 7 | 7 |
| Totals | 11 | 36 | 103 | 139 |

**Source:** Congressional Research Service (CRS), compiled from various news accounts and based on the 1996 *JAMA* published study's case definition for school-associated violent deaths (see discussion above). A similar table presented in earlier versions of this report relied on NSSC data that reflected multiple school-related violent deaths compiled from various news sources, for which a similar case definition was not applied.

[a] The alleged killer's parents were later found shot to death in their home.

Prior to and shortly after the Santana tragedy, the news media reported that similar acts of violence by disgruntled students had been averted because of quick thinking youths who alerted authorities about violent threats that were made by certain students. Notwithstanding, two days after the Santana High School shooting, the *USA Today* newspaper reported six separate school-related violence threats made across the nation, and mentioned a concern that possible "copycat" acts might transpire. Edward Farris, a youth crisis counselor in Los Angeles was quoted as observing that copycat violence is common after high-profile school incidents.[30] On March 22, 2001, two weeks and three days after the Santana High School incident, an 18-year-old male student opened fire with two guns at the Granite Hills High School in Cajon, California, an adjacent suburb of Santee, injuring at least seven people, including two teachers before being shot in the face and subdued by the police officer assigned to the school. A friend of the gunman stated that he believed the shooter was upset because he did not have enough credits to graduate in Spring 2001.[31]

## DRUG ABUSE

Researchers analyzing data from the 1995 Youth Risk Behavior Survey found that students who used alcohol, tobacco, or marijuana on school property reported more frequent drug use than students who used such drugs off school property. Furthermore, students who used those drugs at school were more at risk, than non-drug users, to experience school violence.[32] The *Indicators Study* stated that in 1995, 1997, and 1999, nearly one-third of all students surveyed for the study, who were in the 9$^{th}$ through 12$^{th}$ grades (between 30% and 32%), indicated that someone had offered, sold, or given them an illegal drug on school property, which was an increase from 24% of such students in 1993.[33]

Since 1975, the University of Michigan's Institute for Social Research has conducted the Monitoring the Future (MTF) study. High school seniors and, since 1991, 8$^{th}$ and 10$^{th}$ grade youth have been canvassed annually about their behavior, attitudes, values in general, and substance use. At each grade level, responses of students surveyed were used to represent all students nationwide in public and private secondary schools. In 2001, about 44,300 students in 424 school participated and were surveyed in categories about their lifetime use, past year use, past month use, and daily use of drugs, alcohol, and cigarettes and smokeless tobacco.[34]

---

[30] Scott Bowles, "Violence Threatens Schools Across U.S.: Arrests Made 2 Days After Calif. Shooting," *USA Today,* March 8, 2001, p. 3A.
[31] Todd S. Purdum, "Gunman Fires on School Near Site of Earlier Shooting," *The New York Times* on the Web, March 23, 2001, visited March 23, 2001.
[32] "Use of Illegal Substances Found to Be Related to School Violence," *Criminal Justice Research Reports,* v. 2, November/December 2000, p. 29.
[33] P.Kaufman, et al., *Indicators of School Crime and Safety, 2001,* p. iv.
[34] Daily use of drugs, the MTF report states, usually refers to use on 20 or more occasions in the past 30 days.

MTF researchers reported that results of 2001 surveys concerning drug use among 8th, 10th, and 12th grade students, were mixed, similar to surveys taken in 1999 and in 2000. In 2001, the use of some illicit drugs decreased, while the use of several others remained steady, and a few others showed increases. The use of marijuana, the most widely used illicit drug among all grade levels, remained steady in 2001. There was no change in marijuana usage among 8th graders in 2001, after a slow steady decline in usage since reaching peak rates in 1996. Among 10th and 12th graders, marijuana use remained steady at rates slightly lower than the peak rates reached in 1997.[35]

An increase in MDMA (ecstasy) use was noted in 1999 among 10th and 12th graders, and continued in 2000 and in 2001 among all students, but the rate of increase began to slow. MTF researchers believe that this slowing in the rate of increase results from a sharp increase in the proportion of students who believe that the drug is dangerous. Only 12th graders were asked the question about perceived risk of using the drug. The perception that there is a great risk associated with experimenting with ecstasy increased from 38% in 2000 to 46% in 2001.[36] Additionally researchers found that there was a continuing sharp increase in the availability of ecstasy. The proportion of 12th graders stating that they could get the drug "fairly" or "very" easily, climbed from 40% in 1999, to 51% in 2000, to 62% in 2001.[37] Principle investigator Lloyd Johnston commented that, "[t]his reflects an extremely rapid spread in availability, which is due in part to the fact that this drug is still reaching new communities."[38] African-American students, researchers found, used ecstasy much less than white and Hispanic students. Only 2% of African-American 12th graders surveyed reported using ecstasy in 2000, compared with 10% of both white and Hispanic students.[39] As a matter of fact, researchers reported, "Contrary to popular assumption, at all three grade levels African American youngsters have substantially lower rates of use of most licit and illicit drugs than do Whites. These include any illicit drug use, most of the specific illicit drugs, alcohol, and cigarettes. In fact, African Americans' use of cigarettes is dramatically lower than for Whites, and this

---

[35] Lloyd D. Johnston, P.M. O'Malley, J.G.Bachman, *Monitoring the Future National Results on Adolescent Drug Use: Overview of Key Findings, 2001,* (NIH Publication No. 02-5105), Bethesda, MD: National Institute on Drug Abuse, 2002, p.3-4.
[36] "Rise in Ecstasy Use Among American Teens Begins to Slow," *The University of Michigan News and Information Services,* December 19, 2001, Ann Arbor, Michigan, [http://www.monitoringthefuture.org], visited March 15, 2001, p.2.
[37] *Ibid.*
[38] *Ibid.,* pp.2-3.
[39] *Ibid.,* p.3.

is a difference that emerged largely during the life of the study (i.e., since 1975)."[40]

In contrast to the increase in ecstasy use, other drugs showed evidence of some decline in 2001. Specifically, in 2000, use of heroin among 12$^{th}$ graders reached its highest point since 1975 when the survey began, while such use significantly fell among 8$^{th}$ graders. In 2001, for the first time, 10$^{th}$ and 12$^{th}$ grade students showed a decline in heroin use. Nearly all of this improvement, researchers found, occurred in the use of heroin without the needle (that is, in smoking or snorting the drug).[41]

In 2000, an increased use of anabolic steroids was noted among 10$^{th}$ graders, while such use remained steady among 8$^{th}$ and 12$^{th}$ graders. In 2001, steroid use significantly increased among 12$^{th}$ graders, but showed no further increase among 8$^{th}$ or 10$^{th}$ graders. In 2000, a notable drug use change occurred among 12$^{th}$ graders who showed significant declines in using LSD, crack, and cocaine powder.[42] In 2001, LSD use dropped significantly in 10$^{th}$ graders, but non-significantly in 8$^{th}$ graders. No further change occurred for LSD use among 12$^{th}$ graders. Although both crack and cocaine powder were moderately down from peak levels of use in the 1990s, and far below peak use in the mid-1980s, only use of cocaine powder showed a significant decline in 2001, and only among 10$^{th}$ graders.[43] The use of inhalants, which began to decrease in 1996 from peak levels in all three grades, continued to decline in 2001, but significantly only among 12$^{th}$ graders.[44]

**Figure 1** depicts the usage levels of any illicit drug within the last 12 months by grade level from 1992 through 2001.

---

[40] Lloyd D. Johnston, et al., *Monitoring the Future National Results on Adolescent Drug Use*, p. 39.
[41] *Ibid.*, p.3.
[42] Lloyd D. Johnston, P.M.O'Malley, J.G.Bachman, "'Ecstasy' Use Rises Sharply Among Teens in 2000; Use of Many Other Drugs Steady, But Significant Declines Are Reported For Some," *University of Michigan News and Information Services,* December 2000, Ann Arbor Michigan, p.3 [http://www.monitoringthefuture.org], visited December 20, 2000.
[43] Lloyd D. Johnston, et al., *Monitoring the Future National Results on Adolescent Drug Use,* p.4.
[44] *Ibid.*

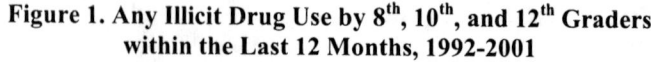

**Figure 1. Any Illicit Drug Use by 8th, 10th, and 12th Graders within the Last 12 Months, 1992-2001**

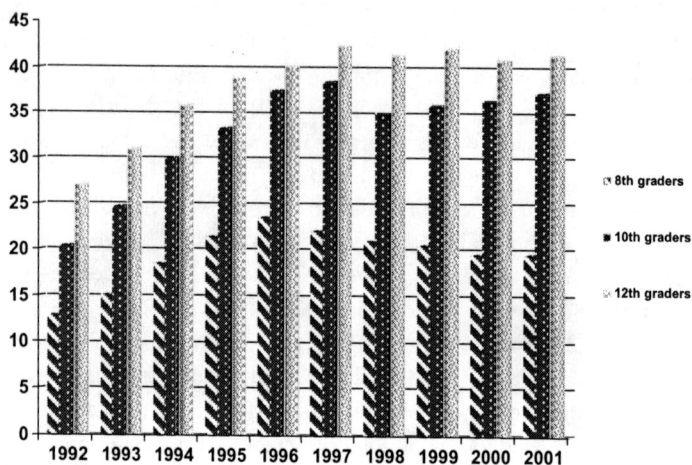

**Source:** Congressional Research Service presentation of data from Monitoring the Future High School Drug Stats Table 2, [http://monitoringthefuture.org/data/01data.html].

In 1998, the use of alcoholic beverages decreased among all three grade levels as students' beliefs about the harmfulness of weekend binge drinking began to change. Also, 1998 was the first year of evidence of a decrease in alcohol use among 10th graders since 1995. In 1997, alcohol use climbed for 12th graders, after slightly declining in 1995 and in 1996. Alcohol use slightly dropped in 1998 for 12th graders, although MTF analysts reported that it was not statistically significant. Among 8th graders, 1998 was the second year for a decline in alcohol use. (See **Figure 2**.) Furthermore, in 1998, one-third of all high school seniors reported being drunk at least once within the 30 days prior to the survey.[45] Lloyd D. Johnston, the principal MTF analyst, concluded that such behaviors of students using both illicit drugs and alcohol tended to change very slowly, and only after young people had assessed the danger in using the various drugs, as well as how acceptable or unacceptable drug use might be to their peers.[46]

---

[45] Lloyd D. Johnston, et al., "Drug Use By American Young People Begins To Turn Downward," *The University of Michigan News and Information Services,* December 18, 1998, Ann Arbor, Michigan, [http://www.isr.umich.edu/src/mtf/pressreleases/mtfnar98.html], visited November 10, 1999.

[46] *Ibid.*

The Safe and Drug-Free Schools and Communities Program 57

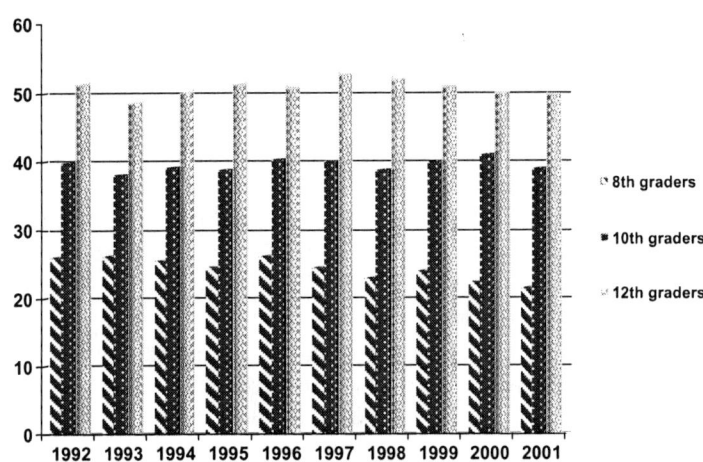

Figure 2. Any Alcohol Use by 8th, 10th, and 12th Graders, within the Last 30 Days, 1992-2001

Source: Congressional Research Service presentation of data from Monitoring the Future High School Drug Stats Table 2, [http://monitoringthefutues.org/data/01data/html].

Note: MTF researchers explained that in 1993, the question asked participants regarding their alcohol use slightly changed. The term "drink" was defined to mean that they consumed "more than a few sips." What the term "drink" meant for students surveyed in 1992 was not indicated. It is assumed that it might have meant to some participants the consumption of a "few sips" of alcohol.

In 1999, researchers concluded that although daily alcohol use declined among seniors, and within the past 30-days use dropped for all grade levels, alcohol use among all teenagers remained at unacceptably high levels.[47] In 2000, teen alcohol use remained relatively stable as in previous years. Almost a quarter of 8th graders surveyed reported drinking alcohol within the past 30 days, while exactly one-half of 12th graders had done so. Also, 1 in 12 eighth graders reported being drunk at least once in the past 30 days, as did one-third of the 12th graders surveyed.[48] In 2001, the rate of 8th, 10th, and 12th graders who reported drinking an alcoholic beverage within the past 30 days prior to the survey were 22%, 39%, and 50%, respectively.[49] Two statistically significant changes occurred between 2000 and 2001 regarding teen alcohol use - a decline among 8th graders who reported having been

---

[47] "Drug Use Among Teenagers Leveling Off," *HHS News*.
[48] Lloyd D. Johnston, et al., "'Ecstasy' Use Rises Sharply Among Teens in 2000...", p.7.
[49] Lloyd D. Johnston, et al., *Monitoring the Future National Results on Adolescent Drug Use*, p. 30.

drunk in the past year, but contrastingly, an increase among 12th graders in daily alcohol use.[50]

Cigarette smoking (defined as smoking one or more cigarettes during the past 30 days), which showed a steady increase all grade levels since 1992, decreased between 1997 and 1998 with 10th graders showing the larger percentage of decline.[51] In 1999, there were no significant changes among all grade levels in cigarette use.[52] Cigarette smoking significantly declined in 2000, among all grade levels. Researchers concluded that the improvements occurring would have meaningful long-term consequences for the health and longevity of this generation of youth.[53] In 2001, cigarette smoking was statistically significant among 8th and 10th graders, but not for 12th graders. (See **Figure 3**.) Lloyd Johnston observed that "These important declines in teen smoking did not just happen by chance. A lot of individuals and organizations have been making concerted efforts to bring down the unacceptably high rates of smoking among our youth."[54]

In 1998, smokeless tobacco use declined more among 10th graders compared with 8th graders and 12th graders.[55] In 1999, as with cigarette use, smokeless tobacco use slightly declined all students, but no significant changes occurred. Researchers observed that the disapproval of regularly using smokeless tobacco increased among 8th and 10th graders.[56] In 2000, smokeless tobacco use substantially declined among teens by an even proportion than cigarette use. Researchers discovered that in 2001, smokeless tobacco use rates remained statistically unchanged from 2000. According to Lloyd Johnston, these rates, however, reflect a decrease by about 40% of smokeless tobacco use by teens peak levels reached in the mid-1990s.[57] (See **Figure 4.**)

---

[50] "2001 Monitoring the Future Survey Released: Smoking Among Teenagers Decreases Sharply and Increase in Ecstasy Use Slows," *HHS News,* NIDA Press Office , December 19, 2001, p. 4, [http://www.nida.nih.gov/MedAdv/01/NR12-19.html], visited February 4, 2002.
[51] "Drug Use Among teenagers Leveling Off," *HHS News.*
[52] *Ibid.*
[53] Lloyd D. Johnston, P.M. O'Malley, J.G. Bachman, "Cigarette Use and Smokeless Tobacco Use Decline Substantially Among Teens," *The University of Michigan Mews and Information Services,* December 2000, Ann Arbor, Michigan, [http://www.monitoringthefuture.org], visited December 20, 2000, p.1.
[54] "Cigarette Smoking Among American Teens Declines Sharply in 2001," T*he University of Michigan News and Information Services,* December 19, 2001, Ann Arbor, Michigan, p.3.
[55] Lloyd D. Johnston, et al., "Drug Use By American Young People Begins To Turn Downward."
[56] "Drug Use Among Teenagers Leveling Off," *HHS News.*
[57] Lloyd D. Johnston, et al., *Monitoring the Future National Results on Adolescent Drug Use,* p. 34.

**Figure 3. 30-Day Prevalence of Any Cigarette Use for 8th, 10th, and 12th Graders, 1992-2001**

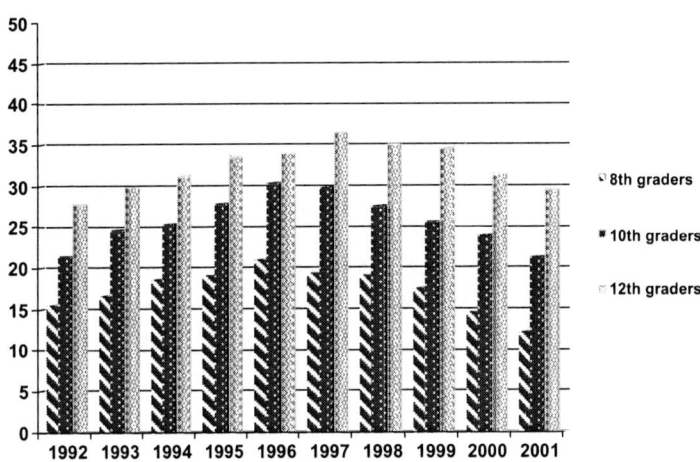

**Source:** Congressional Research Service presentation of data from Monitoring the Future High School Drug Stats Table 2, [http://monitoringthefuture.org/data/01data.html].

Researchers found that there were some demographic differences related to smokeless tobacco use by teens. Such use tended to be higher in the South and North Central regions of the nation than in the Northeast or in the West. Also, such use tended to be more focused in non-metropolitan areas than in metropolitan regions, such use was negatively correlated with the education level of the parents, and tended to be higher among whites than among African American or Hispanic youths. Analysts concluded that one important reason for the considerable declines in smokeless tobacco use by teens in the late 1990s was that a growing portion of youth believed that using the product could be dangerous.[58]

---

[58] *Ibid.*

Figure 4. 30-Day Prevalence of Smokeless Tobacco Use for 8th, 10th, and 12th Graders, 1992-2001

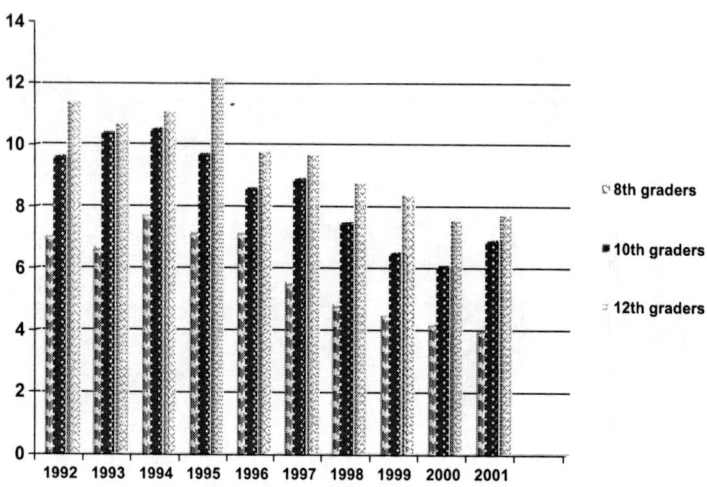

**Source:** Congressional Research Service presentation of data from Monitoring the Future High School Drug Stats Table 2, [http://monitoringthefuture.org/data/01data.html].

## THE SDFSC PROGRAM

The Safe and Drug-Free Schools and Communities Act is a administered by the Department of Education. Grants are authorized for state programs and for a variety of national programs to promote school safety and assist in preventing drug abuse in the nation's schools. For FY2002, a total of $746,750,000 was appropriated for various authorities under the program. Of that total, $472,017,000 was reserved for state grants to support violence and drug abuse prevention programs in practically every school district and community in the nation. For national programs, $34,733,000 was appropriated along with $10,000,000 for Project SERV (School Emergency Response to Violence), $37,500,000 for the National Coordinator Initiative, $100,000,000 for the Safe Schools/Healthy Students (SS/HS) initiative, $17,500,000 for mentoring programs, $50,000,000 for community service for expelled or suspended students, and $25,000,000 for alcohol abuse reduction.

For FY2003, the President has requested $644,250,000 for the SDFSC program. Of this sum, $472,017,000 are requested for state grants and

$172,233,000 for national program activities. This request is a $102,500,000 decrease from the FY2002 appropriation. It would eliminate three activities under national programs - mentoring, community services for expelled or suspended students, and alcohol abuse reduction.

## State Grants

State grants are administered through a formula grant program. Funds for state grants are disbursed as follows: From the total appropriation for state grants each fiscal year, 1%,or $4,750,000 (whichever is greater) is reserved for outlying areas (Guam, American Samoa, the Virgin Islands, and the Commonwealth of the Northern Mariana Islands); 1% or $34,750,000 (whichever is greater) is reserved for the Secretary of the Interior to administer programs for Indian youth; and 0.2% is reserved to provide programs for native Hawaiians. The remaining funds are distributed to the states, the District of Columbia, and the Commonwealth of Puerto Rico by a formula based 50% on school-aged population and based 50% on ESEA Title I, Part A concentration grants for the preceding fiscal year. No state receives less than the greater of one-half of 1% (0.5%) of the total amount allotted to all of the states, or the amount the state received for FY2001. State grant funds in any amount may be redistributed to other states if the Secretary determines that a state will not be able to use the funds within 2 years of the initial award. Also, funds appropriated for national programs may not be increased unless state grant funding is at least 10% more than the previous fiscal year's appropriation.

Of the total allotted to a state, up to 20% is used by the state Chief Executive Officer (Governor) for drug and violence prevention programs and activities, and the remainder is administered by the State Educational Agency (SEA).[59] The Governor may use not more than 3% of the funds for administrative costs. These aspects of the SDFSC program are discussed below.

The distribution of state funds is depicted in Figure 5.

---

[59] P.L.107-110, section 4112 (1).

**Figure 5. The Program Formula to State and Local Schools, 2002-2003 School Year**

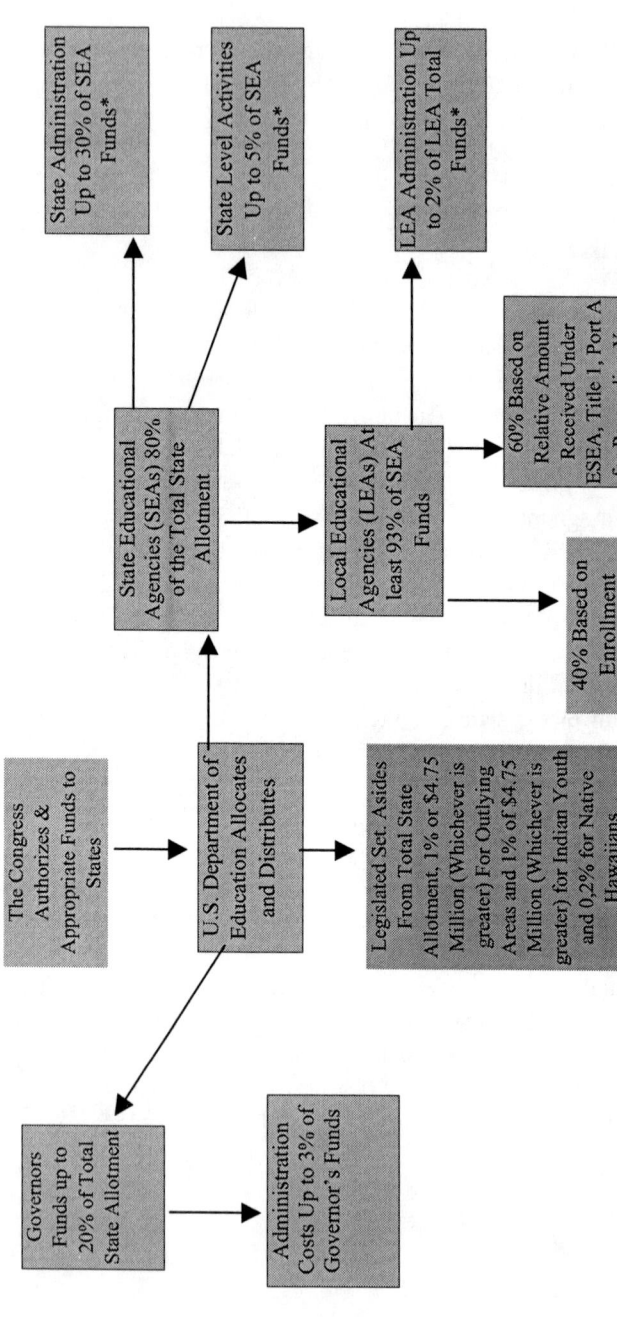

*The sum of these percentage exceeds 100%. States will have to make some adjustments either in Administration or State Activity costs to accommodate LEA percentages.

**Source:** Congressional Research Service. Adapted from Figure 1, "How Funding Reaches States and Local Schools, Fiscal 1995", in the GAO report, *Safe and Drug-Free Schools…* p. 2.

The FY2002 SDFSC state program funds will become available for distribution in July 2002 for the 2002-2003 school year (see **Table 2**).

## State Chief Executive Officer's Funds

As mentioned above, of the total state allotment, up to 20% goes to the Governor to award competitive grants and contracts to local educational agencies (LEAs), community-based groups, other public entities, private groups and associations. Grant and contracts are to be used to support the comprehensive state plan for programs and activities that complement an LEA's drug and violence prevention activities. The Governor must award grants based on the quality of the proposed program or activity, and how such program or activity fulfill the principles of effectiveness.[60]

Funding priority for such programs and activities must be given to children and youth who are not normally served by SEAs and LEAs, or to populations that require special services, such as youth in juvenile detention facilities, runaway and homeless children and youth, pregnant and parenting teens, and school dropouts. In addition, when awarding funds, the Governor must give special consideration to grantees that seek to accomplish a comprehensive approach to drug and violence prevention efforts that include providing and incorporating into their programs mental health services related to drug and violence prevention. Furthermore, funds must be used to implement and develop drug and violence prevention programs that include activities to prevent and reduce violence related to prejudice and intolerance, to disseminate information about drug and violence prevention, and to develop and implement community-wide drug and violence prevention plans. The Governor may use not more than 3% of the funds for administrative costs.[61]

**State and Local Educational Agencies Grant Allocations and Activities**

SEAs can reserve up to 5% of their allotted funds for statewide drug and violence prevention efforts. Funds should be used for planning, developing, and implementing capacity building, training and technical assistance, evaluating the program, providing services to improve the program, coordinating activities for LEAs, community-based groups, and other public and private entities that are intended to assist LEAs in developing, carrying out, and assessing comprehensive prevention programs that are consistent

---

[60] *Ibid.*
[61] *Ibid.*, section 4112(2)(3)(5)(6).

with SDFSC mandated requirements.[62] Such uses of the funds are required to meet the principles of effectiveness (discussed below), should complement and support LEA funded activities, and should be in agreement with the purposes of state activities.[63] Funded activities may include, but are not limited to, identifying, developing, evaluating, and disseminating drug and violence prevention projects, programs, and other information; training, technical assistance, and demonstration programs, to address violence associated with prejudice and intolerance; and providing financial assistance to increase available drug and violence prevention resources in areas that serve numerous low-income children, that are sparsely populated, or have other special requirements. SEAs may use up to an additional 3% of funds for administering the program. For FY2002 only, however, in addition to the 3%, an SEA may use 1% of its allotment (minus funds reserved for the Governor) to implement a uniform management information and reporting system (UMIRS, discussed below).[64]

At least 93% of SEA funds must be subgranted to LEAs for drug and violence prevention and education programs and activities. Of those funds, 60% are based on the relative amount LEAs received under ESEA Title I, Part A for the previous fiscal year, and 40% are based on public and private school enrollments. Of the amount received from the state, LEAs may use not more than 2% for administrative costs.[65] LEAs are required to use funds "to develop, implement, and evaluate comprehensive programs and activities, which are coordinated with other school and community-based services and programs."[66] Such programs should nurture an environment conducive for learning that is safe and drug-free and supports academic attainment, should be consistent with the principles of effectiveness, and should be designed to prevent or reduce violence, the use, possession, and distribution of illegal drugs, and delinquency. Activities should be included to promote parental involvement in the program or activity, coordination with community organizations, coalitions, and government agencies, and distribution of information about the LEA's needs, goals and programs that are funded under the SDFSCA.[67]

---

[62] U.S. Dept. of Education, *Fiscal Year 2003 Justifications of Appropriation Estimates*, p. C-112.
[63] P.L. 107-110, section 4112(c)(2).
[64] *Ibid,* section 4112 (b)(2).
[65] *Ibid.* section 4114 (a).
[66] *Ibid.* section 4115 (b)(1).
[67] *Ibid.*

## Uniform Management Information and Reporting System

States are required to create and maintain a uniform management information and reporting system to provide the public with information about truancy rates, the frequency, seriousness, and incidence of violence and drug-related offenses resulting in suspensions and expulsions in elementary and secondary schools; the types of curricula, programs, and services provided by the Governor, SEA, LEAs, and other fund recipients, and about the incidence and prevalence, age of onset, perception of health risk, and perception of social disapproval of drug use and violent behavior by youth in schools and in communities.[68] The data collected must include incident reports by school officials, and anonymous student teacher surveys.[69] In addition, the state must submit a report to the Secretary of Education (Secretary) every two years on the implementation, outcomes, and effectiveness of its SEA, LEA, and Governor's SDFSC programs, and on the state's progress toward achieving its performance measures for drug and violence prevention efforts.[70]

## *State Application*

To receive an allotment, a state must provide the Secretary with an application that contains a comprehensive plan about how the SEA and the Governor will use the funds for programs and activities that will complement and support LEA activities to provide safe, orderly, and drug-free schools and communities; how such programs and activities comply with the principles of effectiveness; and that they are in accordance with the purpose of the SDFSCA. The application must describe how funded activities will promote a safe and drug-free learning environment that supports academic attainment, must guarantee that it was developed by consulting and coordinating with appropriate state officials and others; must decrease how the SEA will coordinate its activities with the Governor's drug and violence prevention programs and with the prevention efforts of other state agencies and programs, as appropriate; and must comply with several other additional requirements.[71]

---

[68] *Ibid.* section 4114 (c)(3)(B).
[69] *Ibid.* section 4114 (c)(3)(C).
[70] *Ibid.* section 4116.
[71] *Ibid.* section 4113.

## LEA Application

An LEA must submit an application to its SEA that has been developed through timely and meaningful consultation with state and local government representatives, as well as representatives from public and private schools to be served, teachers and other staff, parents, students, community-based groups, and others such as, medical, mental health, and law enforcement personnel with relevant and demonstrated expertise in drug and violence prevention activities. The application should contain, among other things, an assurance that the funded activities and programs will comply with the principles of effectiveness, promote safe and drug-free learning environments that provide for academic achievement, and contain a detailed account of the LEA's comprehensive plan for drug and violence prevention activities.[72]

## LEA Limitation

LEAs are authorized to use the funds for a wide range of related activities. There is a limitation, however, on the use of funds by LEAs regarding drug and violence prevention activities related to (1) "Acquiring and installing metal detectors, electronic locks, surveillance cameras, or other related equipment and technologies"; (2) "Reporting criminal offenses committed on school property"; (3) "Developing and implementing comprehensive school security plans or obtaining technical assistance concerning such plans...."; (4) "Supporting safe zones of passage activities that ensure that students travel safety to and from school..."; and (5) "The hiring and mandatory training, based on scientific research, of school security personnel..." Not more than 40% of LEA funds may be used to support these five activities. Out of the 40% of LEA funds used for five activities, not more than one-half of those funds (that is, 20% of the LEA funds) may be used to support the first 4 activities. AN LEA, however, may use up to 40% of the funds for the first 4 activities, only if funding for those activities is not received from other federal government agencies.[73]

## Principles of Effectiveness for State and Local Grant Recipients

A 1997 study[74] authorized by ED to assess drug and violence programs in 19 school districts across the nation, found that few districts weighed

---

[72] *Ibid.* section 4114(c)(d).
[73] *Ibid.* section 4115(c)(1)(2).
[74] U.S. Dept. of Education, Planning and Evaluation Services, *School-Based Drug Prevention Programs; A Longitudinal Study in Selected School Districts, Final Report, 1997,* by

research results when planning their prevention programs nor generally did they use proven prevention approaches with the greatest potential to make a difference among students. Therefore, to improve the quality of drug and violence prevention programs, ED devised four principles of effectiveness for all grant recipients. On July 1, 1998, the Principles of Effectiveness became operative. Under these principles, grantees are required to use SDFSC State and Local Grants Program funds to support research-based drug and violence prevention programs for youth. The principles were adopted by the Secretary to ensure that SEAs, LEAs, Governors' offices, and community-based groups would plan and implement effective drug and violence prevention programs[75] and use funds as efficiently and effectively as possible.

Grant recipients must:

- Base their programs on a thorough evaluation of objective data about the drug and violence problems in the schools and communities served.

- Design activities to meet goals and objectives for drug and violence prevention;

- Create and implement activities based on research that provides evidence that the strategies used prevent or reduce drug use, violence, or disruptive behavior among youth, and

- Assess programs periodically to determine progress toward achieving program goals and objectives, and use evaluation results to refine, improve, and strengthen the program, and refine goals and objective as necessary.[76]

## National Programs

Under National Programs, funding is authorized for various programs to foster safe and drug-free school environments for students and to assist at-risk youth. These activities and programs are discussed below.

---

E.Suyapa Silvia, Judy Thorne, and Christiane A. Tashjian, Research Triangle Institute, (Washington GPO, 1998), p.5-3.

[75] U.S. Dept. of Education, "Safe and Drug-Free Schools Program," *Federal Register 83*, no. 104, 1 June 1998: p.29902.

[76] Dept. of Education, *Fiscal Year 2001 Justifications of Appropriation Estimates*, v.1, p. D-68.

## Federal Activities

The Safe Schools/Healthy Students Initiative has been funded under the National Program's federal activities since FY 1999. This program is jointly funded with HHS and DOJ to assist school districts and communities in developing and implementing community-wide projects in order to create safe and drug-free schools and to encourage healthy childhood development. For FY2002, and for each fiscal year, the Secretary is required to reserve an amount necessary to continue the Safe Schools/Healthy Students initiative. Other SDFSC National Programs collaborative efforts include funding grants with DOJ's Office of Juvenile Justice and Delinquency Prevention (OJJDP) for projects to recruit and train adult mentors to assist at-risk youth in avoiding alcohol, illegal drug use, participation in gangs, and in acts of violence. Another joint projects with OJJDP is supporting a National Safe Schools Resource Center to provide training and technical assistance to large urban school districts.[77]

Federal activities are authorized to allow the Secretary to consult with the HHS Secretary, the Director of the Office of National Drug Control Policy (ONDCP), and the Attorney General, to administer programs aimed at preventing violence and illegal drug use among students and promoting their safety and discipline. The ED Secretary must carry out such programs directly or through discretionary grants, contracts, or cooperative agreements with public and private entities and persons, or by agreements with other federal agencies, and coordinate such programs with other suitable federal activities.[78]

### *Impact Evaluation*

The Secretary may reserve up to $2,000,000 to conduct a required evaluation every 2 years of the national impact of the SDFSC program and of other recent and new enterprises to deter violence and drug use in schools. The evaluation must report on whether funded community and LEA programs complied with the principles of effectiveness, considerably reduced the usage level of illegal drugs, alcohol, and tobacco, lowered the amount of school violence, reduced the level of the illegal possession of weapons at school, conducted effective training programs, and accomplished efficient parental involvement.[79]

---

[77] *Ibid.*
[78] P.L. 107-110, Section 4121(a).
[79] *Ibid.* Section 4122.

Similar to the required uniform management information and reporting system for states, under national programs, the National Center for Education Statistics (NCES) must collect data to determine the incidence and prevalence of illegal drug use and violence in elementary and secondary schools in the states. Such data must include incident reports by school officials, and anonymous student and teacher surveys. Furthermore, by January 1, 2003, and subsequently, biennially, the Secretary has to submit a report on the findings of the impact evaluation to the President and to the Congress. Along with such findings, the Secretary must provide NCES collected data, and statistics from other sources on the incidence and prevalence of drug use and violence in elementary and secondary schools, as well as on the age of onset, perception of health risk, and perception of social disapproval of such behavior among students.[80]

## *National Coordinator Program*

In FY1999, the National Coordinator Initiative was created under national programs allowing LEAs to recruit, hire, and train persons to serve as SDFSC program coordinators in middle schools. ED officials believed that middle school students were at the age where they were most likely to begin experimenting with drugs and becoming more involved in violence and crime. SDFSCA continues this permissive activity by expanding coverage for national coordinators to serve as drug prevention and school safety program coordinators in all schools with notable drug and safety problems. The coordinators are responsible for developing, conducting, and analyzing assessments of drug and crime problems at their schools and for administering the SDFSC state grant program.[81]

## *Community Service for Expelled or Suspended Students Grant Program*

The Secretary may use national program funds to make formula grants available to states (which include the 50 states, the District of Columbia, and the Commonwealth of Puerto Rico) for administering a new program that requires students expelled or suspended from school to perform community service. Grants would be made to states with 50% of allotted finds based on school-aged population and 50% based on ESEA Title I, Part A

---

[80] *Ibid.*
[81] *Ibid.* Section 4125.

concentration grants for the preceding fiscal year. No state would receive less than one-half of 1% (0.5%) of the total allotted to the states.[82]

The program is forward-funded, which means that funds will become available on July 1, 2002 and remain available for 15-months through September 30, 2003.[83]

### *Grants to Reduce Alcohol Abuse*

The Secretary may award competitive grants, in consultation with the Administrator of the Substance Abuse and Mental Health Services Administration (SAMHSA, within HHS), to LEAs allowing school districts to develop and implement new programs to reduce alcohol abuse in secondary schools. The Secretary may reserve 20% of amounts used these grants to empower SAMHSA's Administrative to provide alcohol abuse resources and start-up assistance to LEAs receiving the grants. Furthermore, the Secretary may reserve up to 25% of the funds to award grants to low-income and rural SEAs.[84]

To be eligible to receive a grant, LEAs must prepare and submit an application to the Secretary containing the following required information –

- Describing activities that will be administered under the grant;
- Guaranteeing that such activities will include one or more of the proven strategies that reduce underage alcohol abuse;
- Explaining how activities to be conducted will be effective in reducing underage alcohol abuse by including information about previous effectiveness of such activities;
- Guaranteeing that the LEA will submit an annual report to the Secretary about the effectiveness of the programs and activities funded under the grant; and
- Providing any additional information required.[85]

---

[82] *Ibid.* Section 4126.
[83] U.S. Dept. of Education, *Fiscal Year 2003 Justifications of Appropriation Estimates*, p. C-121.
[84] P.L. 107-110, Section 4129(a)(d).
[85] *Ibid.* section 4129(b).

## Mentoring Programs

The Secretary may award competitive grants to eligible entities, that is, LEAs, non-profit community-based groups, or a partnership between an LEA and a non-profit community-based organization, for assistance in creating and supporting mentoring programs and activities for children with greatest need. The mandate defines a child with greatest need as "a child who is at risk of educational failure, dropping out of school, or involvement in criminal or delinquent activities, or who lacks strong positive role models." A mentor is defined as "a responsible adult, a postsecondary school student, or a secondary school student who works with a child."[86]

Grants, which will be made available for an obligation of up to three years, may be awarded to eligible entities for mentoring programs that are designed to link children with greatest need, especially those living in rural areas, high-crime areas, stressful home environments, or children experiencing educational failure, with mentors who have been trained and supported in mentoring; screened with appropriate reference checks, child and domestic abuse record checks, and criminal background checks; and who have been deemed as interested in working with such children.

Mentors are expected to achieve one or more of several goals with respect to the children including - providing general guidance; fostering personal and social responsibility, increasing participation in, enhancing the ability to profit from elementary and secondary school; discouraging the illegal use of drugs and alcohol, violent behavior, using dangerous weapons, promiscuous behavior, and other criminal, harmful, or potentially harmful behavior, encouraging goal setting and planning for the future; and discouraging gang involvement.[87]

When awarding grants, the Secretary must give priority to each eligible entity that provides adequate service for children with greatest need who live in rural areas, high crime areas, reside in troubled homes, or who attend schools with violence problems; provides high quality background screening of mentors, training for mentors, and technical assistance in administering mentoring programs; or that plans a school-based mentoring programs.[88]

**Table 2** below provides a 7-year funding history of the SDFSC programs.

---

[86] *Ibid.* section 4130(2)(B)(C).
[87] *Ibid.* Section 4130(b).
[88] *Ibid.* Section 4130(b)(5).

Table 2. SDFSC Appropriations Funds, FY1995-FY2003, by Grant Program ($ in thousands)

| Program | FY1997 | FY1998 | FY1999 | FY2000 [a] | FY2001 | FY2002 | FY2003 Pres Budget Request |
|---|---|---|---|---|---|---|---|
| State Grants | $555,987 | $531,000 | $441,000 | $439,250 | $439,250 | $472,017 [b] | $472,017 |
| National Programs | 0 | $25,000 | $27,003 | $29,023 | $28,000 | $34,733 | $45,000 |
| Project SERV | - | - | - | 0 | $10,000 | $10,000 | $10,000 |
| Coordinator Initiative | - | - | $35,000 | $50,000 | $50,000 | $37,500 | $17,233 |
| SS/HS | - | - | $62,997 | $81,727 | $117,000 | $100,000 | $100,000 |
| Mentoring | - | - | - | - | - | $17,500 | 0 |
| Community Service... | - | - | - | - | - | $50,000 | 0 |
| Alcohol Abuse Reduction | - | - | - | - | - | $25,000 | 0 |
| Total Funding | $555,978 | $556,000 | $566,000 | $600,000 | $644,250 | $746,750 | $644,250 |

**Source:** U.S. Department of Education Budget Service, February 4, 2002.

[a] FY2000 funds reflect the requirement that agencies reduce their FY2000 appropriation by 0.38%. ED rescinded a portion of the states grant appropriation (from the initial appropriation of $445 million by $5.7 million).

[b] The SDFSC is a forward-funded program. For FY2002, as for FY2000 and FY2001, the state grant appropriation was split. Of the annual appropriation, $142,017,000 will become available on July 1, 2002, and remain available through September 30, 2003. The remaining allotment, $330,000,000 will become available October 1, 2002, and remain available through September 30, 2003.

## The Gun-Free Schools Act

The Gun-Free Schools Act, which was Title XIV, Part F of the ESEA, was incorporated as part of SDFSCA because of its close relationship with the SDFSC program. This provision calls for each state receiving funds under the No Child Left Behind Act to have a law that requires LEAs to expel for 1 year any student bringing a weapon to school. The chief administering officer of an LEA, however, can modify the expulsion requirement on a case-by-case basis.[89]

In order to receive funds under the SDFSCA, an LEA must have a policy requiring the any student who brings a firearm or weapon to school will be referred to the criminal justice or juvenile delinquency system.[90]

## EVALUATION OF THE PROGRAM

The purpose of the Safe and Drug-Free Schools and Communities Act under the ESEA prior to its reauthorization was to support, through federal, state, and local programs, the National Education Goal Seven, which was ensure by the year 2000 that every school in the nation would be free of drugs, violence, and the unauthorized presence of firearms and alcohol, as well as tobacco, thereby offering disciplined environments conductive to learning. There were few evaluations of the program under prior law. One assessment of the program's effectiveness concluded that is had failed to meet its stated goal. The National Center on Addiction and Substance Abuse (CASA) at Columbia University[91] concluded:

> A year past the year 2000 deadline and $4.3 billion Title IV federal dollars later, drugs still infest our nation's schools and rates of parental involvement in their children's education remain abysmally low. Efforts to attain Goal 7 - *Safe, Disciplined and Alcohol- and Drug-Free Schools* - have failed and millions of children at schools where drugs are available are in danger of being left behind.[92]

One positive aspect of the SDFSC program observed in CASA's report is the Middle School Coordinator Initiative effort (see National Coordinator

---

[89] *Ibid.* Section 4141(b)(1).
[90] *Ibid.* Section 4141(h).
[91] The National Center on Addiction and Substance Abuse, *Malignant Neglect: Substance Abuse and America's Schools,* Columbia University, September 2001, p. 17-18.
[92] *Ibid.* p.18.

Program above). CASA terms this aspect of the program as one promising initiative for effectively using SDFSC funds. The study stated that "the presence of a full-time prevention coordinator can positively influence both the development of programs and teacher motivation to implement a program curriculum. Active program coordination led to program and careful planning and assessment activities."[93]

In November 2000, a national evaluation of the SDFSC program by ED was released.[94] Surveyors found that the efforts of several LEAs to reduce school violence and drug use through the program were haphazard, and federal funds might be spread too thin. Also, it was found that only 50% of the 600 LEAs canvassed have a definitive goal in place for prevention efforts, such as changing student behaviors or attitudes toward violence and drug use; LEAs with a goal lacked quality data to assess progress; and only 9% had implemented prevention programs based on research. Others used programs like D.A.R.E., which has found by some analysts to be ineffective. The ED concluded that it was questionable to what extent LEAs were complying with the Principles of Effectiveness that require grantees to use program funds to support research-based drug and violence prevention programs for youth.

---

[93] The National Center on Addiction and Substance Abuse, *Malignant Neglect: Substance Abuse and America's Schools,* p. 46-47.
[94] "ED Finds Districts' Drug, Violence Prevention Lax," *Education Daily,* v.33, November 22, 2000, p. 1, 4.

# INDEX

## #

10th graders, 22, 55, 56, 58
12th graders, 22, 42, 54-58
2000 Annual Report on School Safety, 42, 44-46
2002 Annual Report on School Safety, 44
21st Century Schools, 2, 41
8th graders, 54-58

## A

activities for children, 5, 71
administering officer, 6, 73
administrative costs, 3, 13, 32, 61, 63, 64
adolescent(s), 16, 19, 20, 38, 39
African American, 42, 45, 54, 59
after-school programs, 12, 13, 27, 31
age of onset, 3, 65, 69
alcohol, vii, 1, 2, 5, 6, 12, 16, 19, 21, 22, 25-27, 37, 39, 40, 43, 49, 53, 54, 56, 57, 60, 61, 68, 70, 71, 73
all grade levels, 42, 54, 57, 58
anabolic steroids, 55
annual appropriation, 7, 72
anonymous, 5, 65, 69
Anti-Drug Abuse Act, 9, 20, 21, 43
appropriations funds, 7, 72
attackers, 42, 45
attitudes, 25, 53, 74
attorney general, 4, 5, 68

## B

before- and after-school activities, 13, 32
binge drinking, 56
Bureau of Justice Statistics, 45
Bush Administration, 43
Bush, President George W., 43

## C

campus safety programs, 14, 36
capacity building, 4, 63
case-by-case, 6, 73
Center for Alcohol and Substance Abuse (CASA), 24, 73
Centers for Disease Control and Prevention (CDC), 24, 45, 47-50
child guidance professionals, 13, 32
cigarette(s), 42, 58, 59
classmates, 50-52
classroom instruction, 12, 13, 27, 32, 40
close relationship(s), 6, 73
cocaine, 16, 24, 55

# Index

collected data, 39, 49, 69
Columbine, 51
communities, 4, 5, 20, 25, 26, 36, 48, 54, 65, 67, 68
community groups and organizations, 12, 31
community leaders, 13, 31
community service(s), 1, 2, 4-6, 60, 61, 69
community-based groups/agencies/organizations, 3-5, 13, 14, 32, 36, 63, 66, 67, 71
community-based programs, 13, 31
community-wide, 4, 13, 21, 32, 63, 68
coordinating activities, 4, 63
crack, 55
crime(s), 3, 4, 24, 42, 44-46
curricular materials, 10, 26

## D

decision making, 16, 39
Department of Education (ED), vii, 4, 5, 7, 11, 17, 19, 20, 24, 26, 30-32, 35, 37, 39, 40, 43, 44, 47, 49, 60, 66, 68, 69, 72, 74
Department of Justice (DOJ), 4, 41, 44, 47, 49, 68
Departments of Education and Justice, 44
deter youth, 2, 41
disciplined learning environment, 43
discretionary federal activities, 14, 36
discretionary funds, 2, 41
disruptive behavior, 12, 27, 37, 67
district attorneys, 13, 32
District of Columbia (DC), 2, 3, 10, 26, 35, 41, 61, 69
Drug Abuse Resistance Education (DARE), 12, 13, 27, 32
drug abuse violence, 2
drug abuse, vii, 2, 13, 20, 25, 32, 41-44, 60

drug and alcohol abuse, 17, 39
drug and safety problems, 4, 69
drug and violence prevention, vii, 3, 10, 12, 14, 21, 26, 27, 36, 63-67, 74
drug- and violence-free, 13, 31
drug education experts, 39
drug prevention programs, 12, 27, 36, 38, 39
Drug-Free Schools and Communities, 9, 15, 17, 21, 24, 38, 43
drunk, 56, 57

## E

economically disadvantaged, 10, 26
ecstasy, 42, 54, 55
education partnerships, 11, 13, 29, 32
education programs, 3, 12, 20, 25, 27, 64
educational failure, 71
educational levels, 2, 14, 36, 41
Elementary and Secondary Education Act (ESEA), 1, 3, 4, 6, 10, 21, 26, 43, 61, 64, 69, 73
elementary and/or secondary schools, 3, 10, 24, 26, 47, 48, 65, 69
emergency grants, 14, 15, 36, 38
ethnic group, 42, 45
expelled or suspended students, 1, 2, 6, 60, 61

## F

fatal injury, 47, 48
federal funds, 38, 74
federal government, 2, 40, 41, 44, 66
federal, state, and local programs, 43, 73
federally funded program, 17, 39
financial assistance, 64
firearm-related death, 48
fiscal year(s), 3, 4, 7, 14, 37, 61, 64, 68, 70

formula grants, 4, 69
forward-funded, 7, 10, 26, 70, 72
funded activities, 64-66
funding history, 5, 6, 71

## G

gang activity, 12, 13, 27, 40
gangs, 45, 68
General Accounting Office (GAO), 16, 39, 40, 42-44, 62
goal setting, 71
grant recipients, 36, 37, 67
guns, 53

## H

harmful behavior, 71
hate crimes, 5, 14, 36
Hawaiian natives, 14, 36
Hawkins/Stafford Elementary and Secondary School Improvement Amendments of 1988, 9, 21
Health and Human Services (HHS), 4, 5, 7, 15, 21, 22, 24, 25, 42, 44, 47, 49, 57, 58, 68, 70
heroin, 16, 24, 42, 55
high school, 15, 46, 51, 52, 56, 57, 59, 60
high-crime areas, 71
Higher Education Center for Alcohol and Other Drug Prevention, 37
higher education, 14, 36, 37
Hispanic, 54, 59
homicides, 42, 44-46, 48, 49, 51

## I

illegal activity, 32
illegal drug use/use of drugs, vii, 13, 16, 22, 36, 39, 42, 71
illicit drug(s), vii, 12, 15, 16, 19, 22, 27, 38, 42, 54, 55, 64, 68

Improving America's Schools Act, 9, 20, 21, 39, 43
incidents, 42, 46, 49-51, 53
increases in drug use, 16, 39
Indian youth(s), 3, 10, 11, 14, 25, 28, 35, 36, 61
Indicators of School Crime and Safety 2001, 45
inhalants, 16, 19, 22, 42, 55
initial appropriation, 7, 72
innovative approaches, 14, 36
integrated services, 13, 31
intolerance, 10, 12, 13, 26, 27, 32, 63, 64

## J

Journal of the American Medical Association (JAMA), 46-48, 52
judicial officials, 13, 31
juvenile delinquency, 73
juvenile detention facilities, 13, 31, 63
juveniles, 44

## L

Latino(s), 42, 45
law enforcement, 11-13, 27, 29, 31, 32, 45-47, 66
legal intervention, 48
legal substances, vii, 19, 22
legal system, 13, 32
life skills, 16, 39
local educational agencies (LEAs), 2-6, 10-14, 20, 21, 26, 27, 30-32, 36, 41, 62-70, 71, 73, 74
long-term impact, 16, 38
low-income, 64, 70
LSD, 24, 55

## M

major initiative, 2, 41

males, 48
marijuana, vii, 16, 22, 24, 43, 53, 54
MDMA (ecstasy), 42, 54
members of the community, 14, 36
mental health services, 21, 63
mentoring (programs), 1, 2, 5, 6, 60, 61, 71
middle school students, 4, 69
minors, 3
mock trial, 13, 32
model curricula, 14, 36
model drug prevention, 14, 36
Monitoring the Future (MTF), 22, 24, 42, 53-60

## N

nation's schools, 42-45, 51, 60, 73
National Center for Education Statistics (NCES), 24, 42, 43, 45, 69
National Center for Rural Law Enforcement, 5
National Center for School and Youth Safety, 5
national coordinators, 4, 69
National Household Survey on Drug Abuse (NHSDA), 15, 22, 23
national impact, 4, 10, 68
National Law Enforcement and Corrections Technology Center, 5
national leadership projects, 2, 41
national needs, 14, 36
national program funds, 4, 25, 69
national programs, 1-6, 7, 9, 10, 13-15, 19-21, 36-38, 60, 61, 67-69, 72
National School Safety Center (NSSC), 47, 52
native Hawaiians, 3, 10, 61
No Child Left Behind Act, 1, 2, 6, 41, 43, 73
non-profit, 5, 47, 71

## O

Office of Juvenile Justice and Delinquency Prevention (OJJDP), 44, 68
Office of National Drug Control Policy (ONDCP), 4, 20, 68
Office of Technology Assessment (OTA), 16, 38

## P

parental involvement, 64, 68, 73
parents, 12, 14, 20, 21, 27, 36, 52, 59, 66
permissive activity, 4, 69
per-pupil spending, 32
physical conflict, 24, 43
physiological and developmental effects, 39
practical significance, 16, 39
pregnant and parenting teenagers, 13, 31
prejudice, 10, 12, 13, 26, 27, 32, 63, 64
preschool(ers), 2, 13, 31, 41
prevent drug abuse and violence, 2, 41
preventing violence, 4, 21
prevention activities, 9, 10, 13, 16, 19-21, 26, 31, 32, 63, 66
prevention curriculum, 39
prevention programs, 10, 12, 14, 16, 26, 27, 36, 39-41, 44, 50, 60, 61, 63, 65, 67, 74
principles of effectiveness, 36, 40, 63-68, 74
private groups, 3, 63
program activities, 6, 29, 40, 61
program funds, 4, 10, 14, 21, 25, 63, 74
Project Legal Lives, 13, 32
promiscuous behavior, 71
psychoactive substances, 16, 39

public and private entities, 4, 63, 68
public and private nonprofit entities, 13, 31
public and private school enrollments, 3, 64
public schools, 43, 46
Puerto Rico, 2, 3, 10, 26, 35, 41, 61, 69
purposes of law, 14, 36

## R

racial, 42, 45
rate of increase, 54
reduce(ing) drug use, 16, 37, 39, 44, 67
regional centers, 14, 36
Research Triangle Institute (RTI), 39, 67
runaway and/or homeless children and youth, 13, 31, 63
rural and impoverished communities, 5
rural areas, 71

## S

Safe and Drug-Free Schools and Communities (SDFSC) vii, 1, 2, 4-7, 9, 19-21, 25, 26, 32, 33, 38, 40-44, 47, 60, 61, 63-65, 67-69, 71-74
Safe and Drug-Free Schools and Communities Act (SDFSCA), vii, 1, 2, 9, 12, 13, 19-21, 27, 31, 36, 38, 41-44, 60, 64, 65, 69, 73
Safe and Drug-Free Schools Program, 37, 44, 67
Safe and Drug-Free Schools, vii, 1, 2, 9, 19, 20, 21, 25, 33, 37, 38, 40-44, 47, 60, 62, 67, 73
Safe School Initiative, 42, 45
Safe Schools/Healthy Students (SS/HS), 2, 4, 5, 7, 60, 68, 72

safety, 4, 5, 13, 14, 31, 32, 36, 44, 45, 51, 66, 68, 69
school day, 42, 44, 49, 50
school districts, 4, 31, 32, 39, 40, 66, 68, 70
school dropouts, 13, 31, 63
School Emergency Response to Violence (SERV), 2, 5, 7, 60, 72
school grounds, 24, 48
school officials, 65, 69
school personnel training grants, 14, 36
school property, 42, 44, 46, 48, 53, 66
school safety, 4, 5, 12, 20, 21, 27, 43-45, 47, 60, 69
School Security Technology and Resource Center, 5
school security, 5, 66
school shooting, 42, 45, 51
school systems, 14, 36
school year, 10, 24, 26, 42, 46, 49, 51, 63
school-age(d) children, 17, 39, 45, 48, 49
school-aged population, 3, 4, 10, 26, 61, 69
school-aged youth, 12, 27, 43, 46
school-associated, 47, 49, 52
school-based (prevention) programs, 16, 17, 38, 39
school-related (violent) deaths, 47, 48, 52
Schools and Staffing Survey (SASS), 24, 42
school-sponsored event(s), 46-48
scientific rigor, 16, 39
secondary schools, 5, 24, 48, 53, 69, 70
Secretary of the Interior, 3, 10, 25, 61
security guard(s), 52
security technology, 5
seniors, 53, 56, 57
short-term success, 16, 38

smokeless tobacco, 58, 59
smoking, 55, 58
snorting, 55
social and health service providers, 13, 31
social competence, 16, 39
sparsely populated areas, 10, 26
special services, 13, 31, 63
state educational agencies (SEAs), 2, 3, 10-13, 20, 26-31, 33, 41, 61, 63-67, 70
state grant funding, 3, 61
state grants, 2, 3, 5, 6, 10, 11, 15, 19-21, 25, 26, 28-32, 37, 38, 41, 60, 61
state receiving funds, 6, 73
strategies to prevent and reduce violence, 13, 32
street gangs, 42, 44
student hotline, 5
Substance Abuse and Mental Health Services Administration (SAMHSA), 4, 21, 22, 70
substance abuse education, 9, 19, 20, 21
substance abuse prevention programs, 16, 39
substance use, 20, 53
suicides, 45, 46, 48-50
suspending and expelling students, 3

## T

teachers, 12, 24, 27, 43, 46, 48, 50, 51, 53, 66
technical assistance, 4, 5, 10, 14, 26, 36, 63, 66, 68, 71
teen alcohol use, 57
The Gun-Free Schools Act, 6, 73
thefts, 42, 46

threat(s), vii, 24, 49, 52
tobacco, vii, 12, 19, 21, 22, 27, 43, 53, 58, 59, 68, 73
training parents, 13, 31
training school personnel, 36

## U

U.S. Secret Service, 42, 45
underage alcohol abuse, 70
uniform management information and reporting system (UMIRS), 3, 64, 65, 69
uniform management information, 3, 64, 65, 69
using drugs, 2, 19, 41

## V

victim(ization), 12, 27, 46-49, 51
victims of violence, 44
violence, iv, vii, 3-5, 9, 10, 12-14, 19-21, 24, 26, 27, 31, 32, 36, 37, 39-45, 48, 50-53, 60, 61, 63-69, 71, 73, 74
violent acts, 2, 41
violent behavior, 5, 40, 50, 65, 71
violent deaths, 45, 49, 51, 52

## W

weapon(s), 6, 24, 43, 44, 68, 71, 73
white students, 42, 45
world wide web, 37, 40

## Y

young people, vii, 16, 20, 25, 56
Youth Risk Behavior Survey (YRBS), 24, 53